EARTH IS IN SPACE!

(AND OTHER THOUGHTS THAT HURT TO THINK)

JAY NORRY

EARTH is in SPACE!

...and other thoughts that hurt to think

Cover Design & Author Photo: Dawn Norry / Dear23

ISBN-13: 978-1-944916-72-5
ISBN-10: 1-94491672-5

Sudden Insight Publishing
Indie publishing for the Indie Author
www.suddeninsightpublishing.com

EARTH IS IN SPACE!

(AND OTHER THOUGHTS THAT HURT TO THINK)

CONTENTS

FOREWORD

One of the first things honest things I learned from an adult was 'CYA'. That's 'cover your ass', for those of you fortunate enough to have never encountered people who shirk responsibility rather than step up. The principle differs for some of us, but it still applies to all of us. Even when we're making friends or having a chat with one we've already made, we might amend or add something to what we just said after having said it. In conversations I playfully refer to such pronouncements as 'disclaimers'.

In books, it's a bit different. You've got to jump right in with a few words about what the rest of these words will be about, to grab the interest of the readers you're after and push the others away in one carefully worded passage. This is that passage, and I hope you read to the end before deciding if this book is for you. This book began as a blog, and the introduction was much like this foreword.

But this is a book, so we're calling this section the foreword.

Am I making sense so far?

The blog posts were numbered, and those numbers made it into this book. If you want to read about the other subjects I covered in between these, you can find all those other posts on my website; unless some time has passed between me writing this and you reading it, in which case you can find the other books by me that end in '...and other thoughts that hurt to think' and get yourself copies of those. The numbers have been left so they can all be compiled into one giant volume one day; if enough time has passed, you can get that big book. Once you're done reading it, you can use it as a boat anchor.

You see, the more I think about it...the more I realize there are a lot of thoughts that hurt to think out there. Right now I plan on running the blog for three years; that's an easy number to hit, and that many posts means even more chapters. As long as I want to keep these books small enough to fit in your back pocket, we're talking about at least eight adorable little volumes; that ultimate collection I talked about earlier really would be a little unwieldy for the print reader.

If you're not a print reader, you might want to reconsider for this title and the ones to follow. Like I said, they are designed to entertain you on the go; and when I use the word adorable, I do not joke. If you buy and enjoy the ebook version of this, you might want to make sure you get a print copy. The digital empire could collapse any day, after all; and even if it doesn't, having a book like this on your coffee table is a great conversation starter.

Anyway...back to the reason for that blog, which became this book.

Since I was a kid, I have asked questions that got completely different answers depending on who I asked. At first it floored me, that two different people could have two completely different explanations for something I was curious about. Then it freaked me out a little, as I learned there are way more than two sides to every issue. It freaked me out even more when I realized how people treated each other just because they were on different sides of the same issue.

The way personal beliefs determine each of our paths has always been a subject of great interest to me. Any book written by someone who went from little or nothing to great financial or spiritual wealth always points out the importance of examining our own personal beliefs. Successful people know what we believe acts as a kind of blueprint for our outer lives, and that it is very difficult to change the outer without addressing the inner first. Or so they all seem to say.

I have asked a lot of questions of a lot of people throughout my life; and while some of the answers I got were clearly not the highest truth out there, many of the better ones have led me to explore the things a lot of people take for granted a little more deeply.

That's why this book won't be all footnoted up. These are things I've heard, or read somewhere. I did my research, but most of the sources I found to back up some of these ideas were not the same place I first heard them. Many of the original sources are lost, shrouded in the forgetfulness that my questioning mind exhibits sometimes; others are people I have fallen out of touch with, or might not want to be a footnote in a publication of this nature. It would be appropriate for me to mention where I first heard each item, name all my sources, and quote a whole lot of other people at length if this was that kind of book. I've read plenty of those kinds of books, and I understand how the formula works.

This is not that kind of book, however.

This book is about questions many people don't like to ask, and some of the answers I've heard for them over my lifetime. Questions get added as time goes on, just as answers change with new developments and information. That's what this book will cover, the way the people I have talked to about these issues comment on them and feel about them. Since nearly all of my time on Earth has happened in the United States, many of the entries will be things folks in this country believe.

One of the most fascinating aspects of life, to me, is the way beliefs change over time. If this kind of book were written a few hundred years ago, it would undoubtedly mention that the Earth is flat and that the best way to cure most diseases is to drain someone's blood until they get better. They could have footnoted the entries, with lots of quotes from preeminent doctors and scientists… and we would still laugh at them today.

That's another good reason not to mark this book up with footnotes. I don't mind tomorrow's reader laughing at me, any more than I mind today's reader doing the same; but there will be no laughing at my sources, unless you take the time to do some research.

It's entirely possible a little research might just kill that amusement, however; these are thoughts that hurt to think, after all. I happen to believe they hurt for a reason, and that they need to be addressed despite the pain associated with doing so. Just like leeching and horribly inaccurate geography, the beliefs we hold today are not necessarily the beliefs that will be held by the next generation. The one after that is likely to have moved past a lot of this stuff, and the one that follows is sure to assume this entire book is fun fiction.*

Maybe some of this is fiction, and I have collected too much information from unreliable sources. The thing of it is, though…even if some of this stuff is even somewhat true, it's enough to make the most formidable person quake in their boots a little.

And if it isn't true…why do so many people believe it?

There I go again, thinking another thought that kind of hurts to think. Get used to it, my friend…that's what this book is, one fun mostly factual mind-bender after another.

I get it if this isn't your bowl of soup; the most important thing I may have learned in all my questioning is that people are a lot more different from each other than I initially imagined. Riding this beautiful planet around the sun twenty or thirty times is enough to make the most open-minded person realize that life will find a way to push our buttons. It might take more trips to realize those buttons are there so we can address the issues that underlie them and improve our lives through that careful examination; but at that point, it becomes kind of fun to think the thoughts that hurt to think.

Won't you join me? I sure hope so!

Since we will be looking at a lot of

statistics, we'll cover that first. Go ahead and get started on the next chapter, so we can look at how studies show that statistics are often highly misrepresentative of actual facts. And consider getting a print copy, if you haven't already; we designed them to fit easily in your pocket or purse, and whipping out a copy and starting to read might be the best way find out who in the room is comfortable thinking thoughts that hurt to think. They're the coolest people in the room, after all; how great would it be to single them out so easily?

Either way, keep reading! Also, thanks for reading! It was readers like you who inspired this whole giant idea in the first place. When I saw what kind of subjects came up at book festivals and comic cons where I was selling my other books, I knew it was silly to have these thoughts and not share them. I couldn't be more grateful for that inspiration than I am as I encourage you to go on to the next page.

All the best,
Jay

**Also, footnotes can interrupt the flow; and flow is important.*

#001: STUDIES SHOW STATISTICS ARE WRONG!

It's hard to collect information without also picking up some misinformation. The open mind has to learn to be discerning as part of being open, and the curious individual needs to be on guard against filling their heads with things that sound plausible but are actually untrue. One would think we could get accurate information from sources like the news and the government and scientists. Since they deal mostly in information, they must hold truth above all else. Right?

Don't laugh at me; I'm not really that naive.

It's clear that the news on most channels in America is largely opinion, and it's only by watching news from other countries that many people here learn what the United States is all about.

Even those shows have their opinions, but that's fine; it can be good to know what the rest of the world thinks of you, as well as how they feel about you. We know our leaders cook the books to make it look like they are doing a better job than they actually are, and nearly any statistic they put out there is skewed by that perspective.

For example, more Americans than ever now know that unemployment numbers are not real. Once a worker has not been a worker for eighteen months, they stop being counted. They're not considered out of work, even if they've been looking for a job the whole time; they become a non-entity instead, no longer counted or considered. That makes the numbers go up every time layoffs are permanent, eighteen months after that layoff; and has a lot of people thinking that the situation is getting better when it's often getting worse.

Think about it: if 3,500,000 Americans lost their jobs tomorrow, that would be one percent of all of us suddenly out of work. Even if none of those people found jobs in the next eighteen months, the unemployment rate would go right back up to what it was before. We could end up with ten percent American employment at that rate, with only ten percent unemployment rates. If you did it right, you could even end up with both zero percent employment and zero percent unemployment, all at the same time!

Now, that's some tricky math.

Even more tricky is the math we have to do on polls and studies, to see how accurately they represent the actual population. Most people don't have time to take polls, and don't want to subject themselves to being studied. We only get results from a very specific group of people, those with time on their hands and those who don't mind a little poking and prodding. Every study done on sex has to take into account the fact that they're studying an even more specific group than other scientists, since very few Americans are comfortable talking about sex openly with a stranger or having someone take notes when they orgasm.

Then we have to wonder just how honest people are. Answering questions is not always the way to get to the heart of things, since people can say anything they want. Even bodies are bad at telling the truth, since the placebo effect skews a lot of medical studies. It's hard to recommend your product when sugar pills worked better, so a lot of studies don't research or include the placebo results.*

It would be a little embarrassing to admit that placebos work better than pills, when pills are such a great way to make big money.

Scientists seldom get paid to pursue humanitarian projects, with all the funding generally going to whatever it takes to make that big money. They even get busted for skewing their results sometimes, but there are plenty of ways to skew results without breaking the rules.

If your first study group doesn't give you the answers or the results you want, you can always scrap the numbers and get another study group. You can actually do this as many times as it takes, until you can accurately proclaim, "this study shows that whatever I want to say is true." It takes other studies to disprove it; and if they don't get the attention yours did, then more people believe what you said.

It's hard to know what to believe, but it's also hard not to wonder about some of the things being studied. Sometimes experience and observation can teach us more than a scientific journal, as far as learning about life goes.

There will be some numbers in this book, and a lot of talk about those studies I've read or heard about over the years. Although I'm fully aware that it's difficult to get accurate numbers on much of anything, and that many studies exist only to prove other studies wrong; statistics give us some context for many thoughts that hurt to think. I'll share what I've observed as well, when the subject calls for it.

If science and medicine and government continue to change at such a rapid rate, it's highly likely many of the things we believe to be true today will make people a hundred years from now think we were quite the bunch of bumbling idiots. Statistics say Americans have more confidence in their education than any other country, despite the fact that we are steadily falling behind many other countries in the actual quality of education provided. Those are statistics based on the actual testing of knowledge, which is a hard thing to skew…but I can't say for sure…

After all, studies show statistics are wrong!

We won't be discussing any statistics in the next chapter. They hurt the head in a specific way, and we should explore other thoughts that hurt to think in other ways. We'll be leaning heavily on those scientists that we were talking about earlier, but they don't have much reason to be lying about the next topic. They pretty much all agree on some seriously shocking facts, and this is one of them.

Want to know what it is?

Water is alien!

No, really! You see, when the Earth was formed…

Never mind. We'll save that for the next chapter. Go ahead and keep reading if you want to do that now.

**If they do, they're generally in small print at the end of the study.*

#002: WATER IS ALIEN!

When the Earth was first getting started, it was a real fixer-upper. It began as nothing more than a glorified rock floating in space, and grew as more rocks smashed into it and clung together. Once the mass resulting from these collisions got to a certain point, they started attracting bigger and bigger masses. Those masses clung together as well; and after quite some time, they formed a mass that could be called a planet. There were very few of the natural resources we rely so heavily on back then, as most of them were brought here by other chunks of rock floating about in space. Many of the precious metals we mine on our planet are leftover chunks of meteor ore, and much of Earth's topography was profoundly affected by these interstellar collisions.

They didn't just make craters, though; they also filled them. In fact, all of the water that is now on Earth was once somewhere else deep in space. Many of the meteors that strike the planet are little more than giant chunks of ice, which is naturally just frozen water. When the meteors enter the atmosphere, the ice melts and rains down on the planet as water. All of it. That's right, every drop of water in our world once belonged to another world.

At the very least, it belonged to space.

Now, we claim it as ours…just as we claim it is a dwindling resource, all in the same breath.

That's not true, of course. There is as much water on Earth now as there has ever been. In fact…with meteors crashing into the planet rather frequently, we have more water than ever. We also have more people than ever, which is what causes the misperception we call dwindling resources. It doesn't take a mathematician to point out that we aren't working the numbers right, and that the only real problem we have is a lot of selfish parents who just won't stop doing what only parents do.

Actually, that's not quite right. We do have another problem. You know those meteors, the ones that brought us water and gold and copper and tin and all the other stuff we are using up so quickly? They also brought us something else, more than once.

They brought us mass extinction.

See, the Earth is actually on a pretty clear trajectory through space. It spins in both rotation and revolution, finding itself in the same places over and over again. This is a long journey, and one the planet is not making alone. There are countless other objects of various sizes on similar paths, and even more of them on totally different journeys. Most of what's out there are asteroids, the things that brought us water and mineable ore and massive climate shifts. As a result of one or many of these objects crashing into the Earth, the atmosphere of the planet shifted radically enough to support large mammalian life. This shift also caused it to no longer support giant reptilian life.

Those first mass extinctions were good for us, obviously. We had no place among the dinosaurs, just as they have no place in our version of the world. When the smoke cleared from that particular event, there was little left but a few small mammals. They evolved into us, if you believe that sort of thing. Actually, the truth happened whether you believe it or not. The problem is the truth is not always an easy thing to arrive at, particularly when you are talking about stuff that literally happened millions of years ago. Our own recent history is peppered with so many false accounts and conclusions it could be referred to as largely fiction, and science changes its collective mind so often it might be more aptly called science fiction. Who are we to know what happened tens of millions of years ago, we who can't figure out who built the pyramids in Egypt? Or how they did it? Or when, even?

The good news is, all we have to do is stop spending money on killing each other and start focusing on technology to handle this impending event. It is impending, too; make no mistake. There are huge chunks of rock or ice or both floating around out there, just waiting to feel gravity pull them in. It's why we have meteor showers, because we pass through clouds of these things as they float through space to end up here. It's only by chance we haven't seen another the size of the one that made the planet habitable for us in a while, and we're actually right on schedule for another big impact.

Good thing the powers that be have been working on advanced weaponry for so long; they must be prepared to blow it out of the sky when it comes, right?

I mean…isn't that what they've been working on?

If they aren't, they need to get on that. Our social issues don't matter if everyone dies, and there's really no reason to keep killing each other if we're overdue for a mass extinction event.

There's a big rock floating in space, completely capable of doing that for us. Actually, there are more than we can count…and some of them are headed right for us! That's terrifying news, if I ever heard any. Maybe we should call them terrorists, so the folks with all the weapons will train them on our biggest actual enemy.

Of course, options that don't involve counting on the government do exist. Many people have made preparations for doomsday events like giant meteor impacts, and those not directly in its path might stand a good chance of survival.

Originally I would have thought stocking a post-apocalyptic bunker with endless bottles of liquor might be the way to go, should the end come with enough warning to get in the bunker. Lately I have reconsidered, since those emergency quarters are usually pretty tight; the last thing anyone wants is to give up valuable card table space to stacks of boxes filled with bottles of booze.

Fresh air and water are both requirements for this kind of scenario, so maybe the best thing to do would be to make a still for the bunker. Whatever types of liquor you wanted could be blended from bagged or canned ingredients into a mash and allowed to ferment, and then you could have fresh homemade booze any time you wanted. You probably wouldn't want to refer to it as 'moonshine', since that term has traditionally referred to illegal liquor made outdoors under the light of the moon. The word was coined to describe peddlers of this product during what they call 'early prohibition', which brings up a few points most of us know but don't consider deeply because they kind of hurt to think about.

America is still in prohibition era, even when it comes to alcohol. Many counties forbid the creation of these products, others forbid imbibing; and a whole bunch of places have laws against doing either. Moonshiners still exist, in every state. All you need is a container to ferment your mash, and a still to turn it into alcohol. Lots of people make their own booze, even if the practice is illegal; and the ones doing it in dry counties make a business of it, since people still tend to want what they want even when other people tell them they can't have it.

Of course, things would be different in a post-apocalyptic scenario. You wouldn't be a moonshiner, because you would probably not see the moon for the rest of your life even if it was safe to go outside. All your liquor would be made in the shelter you built in case the worst case scenario became your reality someday, probably underground and possibly under a whole lot of rubble. You would probably call it bunker booze, or shelter shine; after all, you need to have some light from somewhere in your shelter to see what you're doing.

Liquor has a history that goes way back, and that bunker booze would be relying on generations of knowledge and experience to come out tasting good and still be able to numb you to your situation. Those of us that enjoy a drink every now and again are glad to have experts in that field, and people willing to dedicate their lives to making the perfect blend or brew for their customers. Having a little more than a passing interest in all this, I found a bit of information I hadn't understood before. See, everything that gets processed in the unique way that leads to any kind of booze all falls under one umbrella. Even if you make it with potatoes or sugar or grain, all liquor is technically a type of brandy.

You might already know this, but it's kind of a fascinating subject even if you do; all booze is brandy, and we'll be talking about that in the next chapter. If you don't need to get on to something else too quickly, you might want to go ahead and read that one too.

#004: ALL BOOZE IS BRANDY!

When everyone was telling me that I was too young to drink, I felt compelled to act out against the restriction. I didn't understand this was a natural reaction to having someone tell you they can do something but you can't; I just knew the other kids in high school were drinking too. 'Keggers' were parties that we usually had in the woods in Montana, even when it was well below freezing. We kept warm by hovering around a bonfire, cuddling with other drunk kids, and drinking from the keg of beer that was often partially buried in the snow.

I liked getting drunk, but I hated the taste of beer. Instead I decided that my drink of choice would be a cheap but popular brand of American whiskey. I would name it, but just typing it out might make me feel a little nauseous. You might be interested to know that this particular whiskey is made in a dry county, which means it's illegal to taste it in the same place it is made; when I found this out, I wondered if maybe that's why the stuff turns out the way it does. If you can't trust a skinny cook, I don't see how you can trust a sober distiller; particularly one forbidden by law from tasting their own brew. Anyway, I'd drink the stuff until I was good and loaded, and then I would keep drinking. It didn't just make me feel tipsy, it made me feel like an adult.

Only they were allowed to drink, after all.

I got to live in Canada for awhile when I was nineteen, and suddenly drinking was not about freezing in the woods or hiding behind a carefully arranged circle of pickups with rifle racks in the back windows. I could go to any bar I wanted, and try any beverage I could pay for. It was the worst hangover I ever had, even worse than the ones I got in high school. When I went from having to hide it to being able to be loud and proud, all in a day, things got pretty out of hand.

As a result, I was pretty much burned out on drinking by the time I reached twenty-one. I was back in the United States, and not impressed by people my age when they hit the bars.

They were acting like a bunch of nineteen-year-olds, to me.

I got into meditation when I was twenty-one, and was all high and mighty about being in control of my consciousness. I didn't drink at all, but I understood at that point why I'd had that relationship with alcohol earlier in my life. Other cultures don't tell their kids they can't drink, and they have little or no problem with this type of acting out. When I realized that my self-control was largely an illusion, and was getting in the way of me having a good time, I considered my options in a new light.

Unfortunately…my options were beer or cheap whiskey, as far as I knew. I didn't even know there were different kinds of whisky, until a good friend insisted I try some.

(It was years later that I realized how to spell the kind of whisky I like to drink, and that even good American whisky didn't have an 'e' in it; but we aren't caught up to that phase of my drinking, just yet. I just thought it would be good to explain why I started alternating between the two spellings.)

I didn't like it at all, and I didn't care for the first two wines he had me try either. The third one tasted like it was made to live on my tongue, though; and it was even better when I swallowed it. Soon I was drinking Merlot like it was going out of style, and soon after I realized it was. My tastes changed, or I got more in touch with them over time; and I ended up settling on drinking a lot of Syrah without feeling like I was settling at all.

That was how I learned that wineries are not full of stuffy or pretentious people, unless you hit the wrong ones. If you do, just keep moving; the wine is just as good at the next place, the people are more fun, and the prices for the same quality of stuff are often much lower. I still love wine, and drink it sometimes... but I have now entered the next phase of the journey that is my drinking.

I've known for quite some time that many brilliant writers of yesteryear were big fans of scotch, and many of the ones alive today are as well. I was scared to try it for the longest time, even though those high school memories had long since faded. It took another good friend to steer me in that direction, and soon I wasn't just drinking scotch; I was studying it. That is actually when I learned the difference between whisky and whiskey, and that they both go through the process of distillation.

Which leads us to brandy. Finally.

See, the process by which all booze is made is pretty similar. Beer and wine have their own way of coming into being, but most spirit production follows a fairly basic formula. It involves a still, a liquid that contains any form of sugar, some temperature to operate that still, and usually some time to age…but when it's done, it all has something in common.

It's all brandy!

A brandy is, by the strictest definition, a spirit made by distilling a liquid that contains any form of sugar. That's a big umbrella.

Vodka is the result of this process, using potatoes and grains. Gin must be made with at least some juniper berries, but it can be made with all kinds of different sugared liquid mixes. Tequila uses agave, but puts it through the same process. Whisky, or whiskey, is made with corn or grain, and sometimes rye.

The kind of whisky I like now must be made from certain ingredients, produced in a certain country, and aged for at least three years before it can be bottled and called scotch. If you're ever looking to gift me something I'll definitely use, any blended or single malt scotch that has been aged at least twelve years will do just fine. Single malt means it all comes from the same place, while blended scotch can be a mixture from distilleries all over Scotland; and some people prefer one over the other. In my experience, my taste buds like a wide variety of this heavenly ambrosia; I don't care if they got the flavor right in one batch or blended a bunch of tastes to arrive at the one they wanted; as long as it's aged long enough, I have yet to meet a scotch I don't like. If you want to really get on my good side when buying me a bottle, the older the better.

Brandy can be made from anything, and we've been over that. However, what we call brandy is really some kind of wine that has been distilled twice; it sits in a barrel for a long time before it's ready to drink, unless you short-cut the process.

Good luck finding a true brandy, for exactly that reason. Brandy starts out around a hundred forty proof, then goes into the barrel. It loses about one percent alcohol for ever year it's in there, and it isn't ready to drink until it gets down to about eighty proof.

As an aside, one proof is one-half percent. Two hundred proof is one hundred percent, which means the strongest booze could never exceed that number. No matter how strong something seems, the math is pretty easy when it comes to figuring out how much actual alcohol content is in there. Just check the proof, and divide by two.

Now, back to brandy…or at least the stuff that says 'brandy' on the bottle. If you get a true brandy, you'll know it. After as much as fifty years in a barrel, the stuff doesn't come cheap. More likely, what you're drinking when you think you're drinking brandy is very young brandy with a lot of distilled water mixed in. That way it doesn't have to sit in barrels for so long that very few people could afford to drink it. To mask the process of watering it down, sugar and caramel are added. That way it looks and tastes more like true brandy.

So, to sum up…

All booze is brandy!

Except brandy, which is generally fermented distilled grape juice that's been heavily watered down.

Alcohol doesn't usually start to pose any problems until we restrict it, and began to mix it with societal pressures instead of cola or fruit juices. There are pretty significant differences between villages and towns, and towns and cities; particularly when we look at the behavior of the individuals living in them.

But I'm getting a little ahead of myself.

We'll talk about that more in the next chapter, which is called...

It takes a village!

Hopefully you have a chance to read it right now; if you don't, you really should get to it soon. It's a good one.

#007: IT TAKES A VILLAGE!

There's that old adage, which says it takes a village to raise a child. There's another assumption about villages, that each of them has their own idiot. But that really doesn't matter right now, since we're talking about a whole different aspect of village life here.

What does matter is that very few people live in villages these days. It's easy to assume we can modify that old saying, and say it takes a town or a city to raise a child, but what if we're wrong? What if the people that made up the saying in the first place were not cautioning us against raising our young in a familial bubble, but were actually warning us of the dangers of raising kids in densely populated areas?

Studies are finally beginning to show what many of us have known all along: parents are not as important as they like to think they are. Children are more deeply influenced by their peers than they are their parents, and modern kids are less dependent on their parents than ever when it comes to actual personal development. It's a good thing, since parents are generally so self-involved and delusional they actually think they're doing the hardest job in the world. What a dangerous myth we have perpetuated, there. It's time to face the fact that where a child is raised is much more important than who does the raising.

Cities are not new, but it may be that the way we lay them out is. Some places really do resemble a series of villages, in some ways; but most modern American cities are made for easy in and out travel, and convenient commuting between neighborhoods. That's great for commerce, but it might not be the best place to raise a kid.

Villages are even older than cities, and plenty of them exist to this day. The only threat to the village is the encroaching city, and the only hope for the city may be a return to the village. That's another scary clock, ticking down along with all the others. While we still have an opportunity, let's have a look at this thing that is supposedly required to raise a child.

Villages are generally small in population, around a hundred to a hundred-fifty people. It makes sense that a group that size would indeed yield an idiot and a genius about once a generation; it turns out they need them both. It's just as important to see that others can screw up even worse than us as it is to see that others can do things we can't do better than we can imagine doing it. When you know both of those people, as you tend to do in a population that size, you don't tease the one and mock him behind his back; and you don't worship the other, or let him do your thinking for you.

Knowing both of those people on a personal level teaches you to have compassion for the one and a healthy admiration for the other. One feeling makes you a better person that learns to be more forgiving and accepting, even of yourself; the other makes you a better person by keeping you both humble and hopeful.

Between the extreme intellectual examples, there are a range of other examples for the young person to learn from in this idyllic scenario. Hunters and gatherers and builders and elders are all accessible to the youth as she or he grows, and a wide range of survival skills are learned long before any child reaches adulthood.

When they do reach adulthood, they go through a rite of passage. They take their place in the community, and are often humbled by the opportunity to provide for the village that raised them at last. They know they'll never be made fun of, or placed on an unrealistic pedestal, or driven out of a social circle; everyone in a village has their place, even the village idiot.

Step it up a bit, size-wise, and you get a town. Do you know what is commonly found in towns, so often there is a saying for that too? It's the town drunk, the guy or gal that no one gives a damn about and that has never managed to learn to give a damn about themselves. We don't get cycles of addiction until we start clustering in larger numbers, and we don't get much in the way of violent crime or theft or psychopathy until a small group is put in place to rule over those large numbers.

Good thing they're so keen on building prisons, and filling them.

Of course, not all societies lock people away for a variety of reasons stated and unstated; some just kill folks they find offensive to the current regime. On the other end of the spectrum, some modern societies have found methods of rehabilitation that actually work.

But that's a subject for another day.

Surely the two topics have nothing to do with each other.

Villages often pass the time in fun activities in which there is no winner or loser, and in which participants learn or hone valuable life skills. In their attempt to imitate this self-esteem building model, American schools have done exactly the opposite. They have modified games with clear winners and losers to be purposeless, and the only lesson kids are learning is that they get rewarded no matter what they do. These aren't children that know how to hunt or fish or garden, like their counterparts in these villages; these are kids that need to be taught to compete, since that's what is waiting for them in the world they're not being prepared for.

I mentioned hunting, fishing and

gardening for a reason. It has seemed both obvious and important to me for a long time to stay somewhat in touch with the process that feeds my body. People in villages are way more aware of the process than I am, at least experientially; but that doesn't mean I can't see how being out of touch with where our food comes from has made us quite a bit different than them. After growing up in a rural area, I moved to a more populated spot to begin my adult life. I was a little shocked at how a lot of the people I met felt about hunting, and was completely unsurprised to find that urban attitudes about such things were full of consequences folks in the country don't have any trouble dealing with.

We'll talk about what hunting has done to help and hurt our country in the next chapter. We'll also talk about the dangers of engineering hunting laws that give certain wild animals the deadly combination of few predators and little prey. There's more to it than I pretend to understand, but I do know one thing that freaks me out a little…

They're eating our pets!

#008: THEY'RE EATING OUR PETS!

I don't begrudge spending about half my childhood in Montana, or try to pretend it never happened. Many of the lessons cities had to teach me in adulthood were put in a certain perspective given that rural upbringing, and I wouldn't trade what I have learned from both to only have a mind full of memories from one. Country life has different things to teach than city life, and I continue to feel they each have a lot to offer. Even if the main thing we learn by changing our environment is that people vary a lot more widely than we once supposed, it's a valuable lesson to learn.

One of those variances is how food is viewed, in the many stages it must exist before it makes it into a person's belly. It was strange to move into an area where almost no one I met had any experience in hunting or gardening, as was realizing how many people found one repugnant while seeing the other as a hobby usually dedicated to growing flowers no one ate.

During the decades I have lived in or near large cities, this awareness has shifted considerably. On one hand, there are more food gardens in American cities now than there were back then; people have gotten interested in organic produce, and the only way to really guarantee all the ingredients used to grow your fruits and vegetables is natural is to do it yourself. Labels can be misleading, as can words like 'organic'; but we'll talk more about that later.

Right now, let's talk about hunting.

If you don't eat meat, this still relates to you. Even if you don't eat any kind of meat-related products, this relates to you. If you grew up without ever once eating meat, and have always eaten only food that your family cultivated…first of all, you're probably pretty low on the micro-nutrients that many of us built up in childhood and which later made it easy for us to go vegetarian or vegan for awhile. Second, this still relates to you. Even if you are living the ideal vegan lifestyle and managing to stay healthy, you are only doing so by eating life. It's how things work, here on Earth.

I'll go you one further, and acknowledge there is such a thing as a fruitarian...if you'll acknowledge that you would rather be plucked in your prime and eaten rather than left to live past your physical peak in peace. Plants have an emotional life, just like people and animals; the fact that we can't hear their protestations as we take their life doesn't mean they aren't trying to give them voice. It's why other plants around them act defensively, and go so far as to change their chemical makeup to ward off predation with bad taste or thorny spines or poison. They have their own version of wailing in pain, and the fact that we can't hear the screams of lettuce as it gets consumed doesn't mean it isn't happening.

The truth is, nobody likes to be eaten.

Be that as it may, life must eat life. At this point it comes down to the way our food lives before it dies, and the question shifts logically to whether it is better to be farmed or free before it becomes someone's meal. Even if it's free, it will eventually become someone's meal: a predator will take it down, or a scavenger will pick its bones clean, or flies will lay eggs in it that become hungry maggots whose primary diet is rotting flesh.

Gross, right? It's true, though; even taking the essential fluids from a corpse to make sure it doesn't come back to life and locking it in a box to keep it from returning if it does only forestalls the nasty encroachment of decay. Mostly, it just keeps the dead from coming back to life.

The money that has saved a number of countless species from extinction in the United States has come largely from hunting tags. These tags are issued in certain areas where the populations of specific species have expanded beyond the sustainability of their environment. Traditionally, the tags have focused on balance: that means issuing a set number of tags for predatory animals, and for species certain people don't think it's right to hunt.

That's why, when a mountain lion or wolf or coyote are caught and examined near urban areas in America, their bellies are invariably full of the flesh of domestic dogs and cats. Chickens get eaten, too; but most people here eat them on a regular basis, so it's hard to get folks riled up about that. We all have a list in our minds, which tells us some animals are edible while others are our friends. The list may be different in other cultures, but they still have a list; and they might be just as disgusted by what we eat as we may be by their diet.

Also, they aren't a danger to our pets; wild predators are.

The less we let hunters do the job they have quietly and thanklessly done almost since the beginning in our country, the more our pets will get eaten by animals that are not being hunted anymore. The more steps we put between us and our food, the more questionable that food source invariably becomes. There are undoubtedly good reasons why laws exist preventing the people eating factory farmed food in America from seeing inside those facilities, while millions of Americans watch hunting shows on television and on-line.

Maybe you don't think people should keep pets, or maybe you think it's no big deal when one gets eaten. Forgive me if I don't freak out when this gets to the point where other people's children are being eaten, then; I'm much more attached to my pets than I am to their kids, and there are a lot more kids in this country than we need grownups tomorrow to hand it over to. And make no mistake: if we don't handle the human or the predator overpopulation problem, these problems will inevitably interact in the most horrifying fashion.

One last thing to ponder, maybe two.

First, elk and deer meat are some of the most healthy and delicious foods out there. It can be argued their freedom causes that, or that nature has designed the most challenging hunt to be the most nutritionally rewarding. Neither point matters nearly as much as the first one.

Second, many animals eat babies. Black bears are notorious for seeking out baby black bears when they come out of hibernation, because they know baby bears to be easy prey. If they'll eat their own babies, you can be sure they wouldn't hesitate to eat ours.

We don't have to worry about people eating their babies until they find themselves starving with no hope in sight. There were signs in Russia when socialism was as its peak presence there, reminding people it was wrong to eat their babies. I guess hunger brings out the worst in everyone. Or maybe black bears are just good socialists.

Many people may believe we should leave wildlife alone, and let a natural equilibrium somehow occur on its own beyond the borders of our cities. The ecosystem doesn't work that way, however; we need rural areas to provide food for the urban sprawl, and we can't have vegetable farmers running from mountain lions every time they walk out on the field. Also, we are part of this ecosystem; like it or not, we are going to have an impact until we go extinct or leave the planet en masse. Why not make that impact deliberate and conscious?

Vegans and vegetarians are only avoiding taking animal life if they grow all their own food, and don't use any pesticides or herbicides; otherwise those fruits and vegetables get farmed, and insects lose their lives constantly in the process. Deer fawns often get chewed up in tractor teeth when harvest comes, and that blood is on the hands of every person eating food from that farm. Insects may not be real high on the list of animals we want to protect, and many vegans won't hesitate to smash a spider or swat a fly;

but are we really so far removed from life that we don't recognize it when we see it? If you will kill a mosquito without hesitation, what moral protest can you really put forth against hunting?

Whatever sense of moral superiority anyone gets from eating only fruits and vegetables from their own garden is a false one, anyhow; life eats life, and very few of us find a way to get around that rule completely. Food from your garden is super good for you, especially supplemented with meat from the forest; but eating it doesn't make you ethically better than anyone else consuming life to live. Even if you believe some enlightened people don't eat any type of physical sustenance, they always claim to be consuming cosmic energy. They also always say they did it to prove a point, or to set an example.

The rest of us...well, we eat food. Also, we kill the things that will eat us even if we don't plan on eating them. We kill the animals that threaten our livestock, our children and our pets. Otherwise, they kill us. It's just how life works: either we eat them, or they eat us.

Welcome to Earth.

#010: THAT'S A BIG DAM PROBLEM!

A while back, my little family found ourselves under an evacuation order. There was a dam having problems upstream from us, and our town was one of the places in danger of being flooded. It was a real worst case scenario they were entertaining, and the proper steps were taken to avoid that possibility…but it got me thinking, and doing a little research. It's amazing how many things come to your attention when you're writing a blog called 'Thoughts that hurt to think' every week, and the universe has spoken to me in a number of ways to bring me fresh ideas.

Honestly, though…I never thought I would get an automated phone call telling me it was time to evacuate. Being the person I am, I started asking some questions. It turns out this is one of the best examples of thoughts that hurt to think I could possibly come up with, and I may never have thought of it if we hadn't been evacuated. Now I wanted to know what that worse case scenario was, how likely it is to happen, and what measures are being taken to avoid it.

It turns out catastrophe is coming, that it's inevitable, and not much is being done about it at all. If you think I'm being dramatic, read on…then do your research, and see if you still disagree.

Here's what I found out:

Pretty much all the dams in America were built somewhere between the 1930s and the 1970s. They provide power and water allocation, create recreation areas, and make places that used to be river bottoms or flood plains inhabitable. We all know that, right? What I didn't know, until recently, is that all the dams in America were built to last around fifty to a hundred years. Do you realize what that means?

That's right, I'm about to do some of that author math; please be kind, and cut me a little slack. I'm supposed to be imaginative, and dramatic…precise mathematical accuracy comes in third at best.

If the last of the dams were built in the 1970s, even the youngest dams in the country are nearing fifty years old. The ones built in the thirties are only a couple decades from expiring, according to the very people who designed them. The Oroville dam is the tallest dam in the United States, and has technology that senses the amount of pressure each level of the structure is experiencing; that technology was built into the dam, which means it is as old as the structure itself.

Which is to say, my iPhone probably has more advanced technology than the tallest dam in the country. Do you know how many times technology has doubled in virtually every field since the infrastructure in America was built? Are there dozens of other things right before our very eyes, that were only designed to last until right about now? Were they relying on us knowing that, and replacing it with the far superior ideas of a future they could only imagine?

If so...someone should probably come up with a solution, and fast. Or a bunch of them, preferably. If all the dams burst in our country, the number of homes that would be destroyed or rendered uninhabitable is pretty mind-blowing. And that's the thing…they're designed to last fifty to a hundred years, and fail. Oh, and also…time's up! It only took a few years for folks to start building in those fertile new valleys, and recreating in those beautiful new lakes. Now the structures that created those lakes and valleys are old, and rickety; and apparently that's how they were designed. To last until right about now.

Now, that's a big dam problem!

Here's another one: how do you build a new dam, to replace the old one? Do you place it downriver, or up? Do you displace a bunch of households upstream, or a bunch of households downstream? It seems pretty clear we can't rebuild them where they stand, while they're full of water and still doing the jobs we depend on them to keep doing. Was there a plan for all this, back when this relatively temporary fix was implemented?

These dams are part of the infrastructure of our country, and they provide more than recreational areas and building sites. They also provide power, and lots of it. They distribute water to the areas that need it, when they need it, by holding water in reserve during rainy years and releasing it during droughts. It's really a great system, one we have come to depend on in so many ways a failure would have butterfly effects that would flap in nearly everyone's face.

By the way, I didn't randomly choose the Oroville dam just to make an example of it; that's the one that was having problems, which called for my family to be evacuated for a couple days. Nothing happened, ultimately; except a whole bunch of people were displaced and a ton of hotels and motels in nearby safe zones made a nice little pile of money. After a couple days the news announced it was safe to go back, which meant it had been safe to stay there the whole time. They called it the largest evacuation in American history with no incident, but I soon took to calling it the biggest false alarm in American history.

Funny, right?

Although we have some of the nicest weather in the country, people in this state still tend to obsess a bit over annual rainfall. When we don't have enough, signs go up in fields questioning the morality of how this precious resource is being allocated;

and when we have too much, we do things like orchestrate the biggest false alarm in the history of the whole country. We have to take a larger view of the state to begin to appreciate how much good stuff starts here, though; so let's do that.

Just about everyone knows California is in a constant cycle of years of drought followed by massive rainy seasons followed by drought followed by endless repetitions on the theme. It's the dams and dikes and levies that keep us from running out of water during those droughts, and those things are apparently not built to last. As much as some folks in other parts of the country might claim they wouldn't miss the state if it slipped quietly into the ocean, others know California produces much more than movies and microchips.

With the largest economy in the country, the state ranks in as the sixth largest economy in the world. California represents around 13% of all the commerce in the United States, which is pretty impressive considering how many states provide less than one percent. I thought most of the country's food was grown in the midwest, even when I first started living in California; it took moving to the northern part of the state for me to realize America depends on it for far more vital things than entertainment or technology. The state quietly and thanklessly produces over 90% of the country's broccoli, garlic, plums, kiwis, celery, walnuts and artichokes. If you look at the list of fruits and vegetables that California produces over fifty percent of, it gets a little ridiculously long.

The American diet would be reduced pretty quickly to little more than grains and meats, if California was not around. Even the fruits and vegetables other states produce to compliment the massive supply that comes from California would suddenly become the most expensive item on everyone's shopping list, and the meat market would skyrocket right along with it if California's farms all disappeared. With such a bland diet, maybe no one would care they didn't have any new movies to watch; even if they still had plenty of corn to pop.

If we're all in this together, and it's probably best if we are, it might be a good idea to get this infrastructure thing figured out. California only has around

1400 of the 84,000 dams in America, and its economy is more likely to help those other states rebuild than the other way around. Rather than point fingers at each other, we might all benefit from acknowledging our lives wouldn't be the same if not for the efforts of a lot of other people. It's easy to forget how much you depend on others when those benefits are still around, and it's almost impossible to avoid being trapped in a set of beliefs that are built more on ignorance and opinion than knowledge and facts.

Which, coincidentally, leads us to the topic of the next chapter. If you have a few minutes to read it as well, I'll explain right at the beginning why I gave it such a silly title. One of the best ways to look at heavy subjects is through the lens of humor, in my opinion; and this is definitely a heavy subject. Each of us can only gather so much information from the point of existence we see things from, and our minds are designed to start forming beliefs around a variety of subjects long before we can possibly know everything about any one of them.

The next chapter, therefore, is called...

Everybody lives in a bubble! Bubble!

#011: EVERYBODY LIVES IN A BUBBLE! BUBBLE!

When I was a kid, my dad made it clear in many ways that being a broad-minded person has a lot of benefits. Mostly, it was by setting an example I didn't appreciate until I got older; but sometimes he made a real effort to hammer a lesson he had learned into my thick skull, and there's really only one way to do that. You've got to remind a person, over and over, that certain things are not to be taken for granted…even if the person you are reminding is yourself.

My dad used to say it, whenever the occasion called for it; and over the years I've made it a practice to continue pointing it out to myself.

"You live in a bubble!"

That's what he used to say to me, back then; and that's what I say to myself, now.

As a kid I was more apt to talk back than I was to learn, which is really not that much different than the way I am now. The more I heard the phrase, the more I longed for a good comeback. Finally, one day, I found one.

"If I live in a bubble," I said to my dad, back in the day, "then you live in a bubble too!"

He didn't hesitate, and I hadn't considered he might have the perfect comeback to my perfect comeback already thought out.

"Of course I live in a bubble!" he shot back. "Everybody does!"

It has been helpful, to remember that lesson. I originally had it in the queue for the blog, under the title 'Everybody lives in a bubble!'; since it certainly qualifies as a thought that hurts to think. Then my favorite pop star came out with a song very much about this very thing, and I changed the title a little and released it under the title I also used for this chapter. So…thanks to my dad and Katy Perry, here we are.

One of the best ways to broaden our horizons is by reading books, and the written word can do a fine job of informing us about other parts of the world and other ways to think. Once you read enough, though, you're going to realize there's really nothing like traveling to other places to open your eyes to how others live. Walking new streets and seeing new faces helps keep us somewhat in touch with how it feels to be around the wide array of folks we share a planet with, even if we seldom speak a common tongue. It doesn't always make us feel worldly to practice this, however; often it can make us even more keenly aware of the fact that we live in a bubble.

So, what does it mean to live in a bubble? Is there any way around it?

Well, no. That's why I felt so confident calling this chapter 'Everybody lives in a bubble! Bubble!' instead of 'Most of us live in a bubble! Bubble!'; because this is just the way our brains are mapped out. It's not a bad thing, really. I mean, the only way you can say you don't live in a bubble is if you see everything and know everything; even then, you might be the one most keenly aware of the fact that you live in a bubble.

A bubble of omniscience!

I can't speak to that, but I can speak to the existence of my own bubble. My family moved a few times when I was a kid, and I remember how different Arizona was from Oregon was from Montana. Visiting extended family in California had me wanting to live there, and now I do. It probably won't be forever, though; as nice of a bubble as it might be, my wife and I both enjoy changing things up and expanding our shared comfort zone. With so many places in the world to see, and how much we both love to travel, it's not impossible to see us calling somewhere else home.

That's the other thing…traveling is great, and it certainly expands the size of your bubble; but you've got to live somewhere to get a real feel for the place. I spent quite awhile in Canada, some time back…even speaking the same language, I was lost at first trying to fit in. And they're really nice people; I can't imagine what it's like coming to America, with grumpy guys like me to welcome you with a bunch of slang that barely even makes sense to me.

You can't know what it's like to only live in one place and really plant your roots there if you travel a lot. The person constantly on the move lives in their own bubble, even if that bubble is traveling the world with them. The person dedicated to their favorite chunk of land is just as correct in doing so as the person trotting around the globe; and they have as many ways to expand their bubble.

I hate to state the obvious, since I'm such a big fan of hers, but even Katy Perry lives in a bubble. Her awareness of it doesn't pop it, but it might help the rest of us be a little more aware of ours.

The truth of the matter is that you live in a bubble, your family lives in a bubble, science lives in a bubble, and politics definitely lives in a bubble. Much like your home, you might want to customize your bubble to fit your needs and make sure it doesn't cause you too much discomfort; other than that, the best thing you can really do is get used to living in a bubble.

Bubble.

Speaking of bubbles…

Many people in America refer to a certain percentage of the folks outside their bubble by their financial slice of the pie graph we all fall into. They call them 'the one percent', and use all kinds of demeaning phrases to characterize everyone that falls into that category. There is a question we need to ask before we can start passing judgment, however; and that question is both the title and the topic of the next chapter.

#013: ONE PERCENT OF WHAT?

Sometimes the only way to be right about something is to start out being wrong about it, and work your way from there. So it was with the one percent, and me. I had heard people refer to the ultra-rich with that term before, and probably misused it a few times, before I gave it a little more thought and did a little actual research. What I found put things into perspective, and made me wonder if I had been the only one that didn't know these things.

For example: if you make thirty thousand dollars a year in this country, you are in the top one percent of the world's earners. What we consider poverty, or courting it, many other countries consider great wealth. Or at least a good living. If you're not making over thirty thousand dollars a year and you live in America, you might want to consider another line of work. Life is not getting any easier for low income households any time soon. There is still opportunity for good work and good pay in our country, even if we have to work harder for it than ever.

Here in America, the top one percent of earners are mostly artists and entrepreneurs. Over ten percent of Americans will find themselves in that category at least one year of their lives; that's hardly an indication they are on the path to hoarding diamonds like a dragon or drafting up their manifesto to dominate the global marketplace. In fact, most of us are doing our best to be one of the ten percent that gets to be one of the one percent at least once in our lives; and we're always happy to see our friends and loved ones move towards or into that category.

These are not the people we mean, when we refer to the one percent. We are talking about the people who are born into more money than the human mind can get a realistic grasp on. We're talking about the royal blood of our country, the people who have so much cash the only thing that will often get them excited is the opportunity to rule. So that's what we let them do, since none of us have the time or the money to play the game their way. These folks are more accurately described as the one percent of the one percent, and they have more streams of income than any honest business person could ever hope to.

Also, they aren't bound by the same laws...although they are somehow the ones writing them. Our recent history is peppered with public examples of how our legal system is for sale even to citizens, and unwilling to put politicians in the same prisons they built to put those they served in.

Served...that's a funny word, isn't it? How are we to feel served by people who make more money than almost all of us, have the best healthcare there is, and are immune to prosecution for their public crimes? Lots of words come to mind when I think of those who claim to serve us, but service is not one of them.

As unemployment rates rise despite claims to the contrary, and more and more Americans live on the streets with each year that passes, it's easy to see how generations coming up are not showing much interest in leasing the American dream. Many of them even resent the one percent, without giving them props for working so hard to get there. They don't seem to understand that it's the one percent of the one percent that are shifting the balance of wealth and power further away from them with each day they spend not learning to be a person of value in some marketplace or another. The one percent are there to give those of us working hard every day hope. They're not the ones who want to take without giving; the majority of the one percent are looking to trade value for value, and ensure both parties get the most from each transaction.

So…you're in the one percent of the world, if you make thirty thousand dollars a year. Twenty percent of American households earn over fifty thousand dollars a year, and ten percent earn over a hundred thousand. You only have to make about a half million dollars in a year to be in the one percent, and that hardly constitutes a lifetime's wealth in modern America. Those in the lower ninety-nine of the one percent will probably have to keep working next year, while the folks we're talking about never really had to. The one percent of the one percent in America is actually the one percent of the one percent of the one percent of the world. The honest truth of the matter is most of us will never hang out with one of those people, and many folks wouldn't want to.

What would you talk about, anyway? How hard it is to find a bank that will print checks big enough to write in all those zeros? What a pain it is to rule the world, and try to play it off like you're being of service?

The truth is most of us don't have much in common with these folks at all. That's why they're the one percent…of the one percent, of the one percent. The actual one percenters aren't so bad, in my experience.

Some people think the issue of wealth distribution is enough to drive a person to drink; others go so far as to blame this sort of thing for most or all addictive drug use. Like rats in a cage versus their counterparts in fun and free settings, maybe we don't feel the need to use if we feel a certain sense of freedom.

Factor in how many people have several prescriptions, and let that stew.

Now we're looking at a population that is largely under the influence of one mind-altering substance or another, and we aren't even counting the sugar and caffeine so many of us take in regularly.

But, really...it's no cause for alarm.

The truth of the matter is that we have no alternative to drug use; it's part of our own chemical makeup, and one of the most interesting aspects of what makes us who we are.

So, relax...and don't worry. Spark up, or drink up; and remember what it's all about in your own special way. Then read the next chapter, where we talk about how...

We're all on drugs!

#015: WE'RE ALL ON DRUGS!

The most strict definition I ever heard for 'drug' stated that any substance you put in your body by any means is a drug. At the time I argued food shouldn't be considered a drug, and air and water shouldn't either. My view was that a drug should be classified as something which alters your consciousness in some way, and that most people probably think of mind-altering substances when they think of drugs. I have since realized both arguments were pretty much right and pretty much wrong all at the same time.

One of the things I didn't realize, when I first learned what drugs were, is that it isn't the drug itself that has those mind-altering effects. Substances create chemical reactions inside our bodies, and they are what make us feel sharp or dull or paranoid or euphoric. Those same chemical reactions can happen without the substance, as has been proven time and again by the placebo effect; but they can't happen without the receptors for those substances, or without the chemical reaction caused when the two interact.

Much of the food we eat has way more powerful stuff in it than we might think. We're talking about leaf lettuce and vegetables, not that other stuff often mistakenly referred to as food; we'll address that next, since we clearly need to. Most natural foods have something in them that will alter your consciousness at least a little bit if you consume enough of them, but those are chiefly vitamins and minerals interacting with their associated receptors in our bodies. Being healthy comes with its own euphoria, and that reaction is there to bring us back for more of the good stuff. But there are also a lot of natural foods that contain significant levels of DMT, or dimethlytryptamine. That is considered to be the most potent psychedelic there is, and is categorized as highly illegal by the folks with all the best weapons and prisons in our country.

Before you freak out and start checking labels, you should know that your body is actually one of the best manufacturers of this substance in the world. DMT is in all of us, and we all trip on it regularly. Where do you think those wacky dreams come from? There are other chemicals in our bodies, which inhibit the effects of this powerful drug in most of the things we eat and in most of our waking hours. Animals that don't have these inhibitors trip hard when they eat some of the foods people consider completely harmless, and a few of them will even keel over and die. It's like putting sugar in a car's gas tank: once it hits the engine, that's all she wrote.

You knew I was going to mention sugar eventually, right?

We make all kinds of things from the raw materials we find on this planet, and for some reason we seem pretty obsessed with putting more of them in our mouths than we should. Sugar in the raw has lots of vital nutrients, and it really is a healthy part of a balanced and natural diet. It is not, however, what most folks in America think of when they think of sugar. That's been refined, which is a strange label to put on a process that takes out all the good stuff and makes it a point to add bad stuff. It's also been replaced in a lot of instances, with something called high fructose corn syrup.

Unless you have been living under a rock for some time, you know the dangers of consuming this stuff. If it isn't the devil itself, it was certainly cooked up by one. There's really no clear reason why this product was even developed, unless you leave arguments about nutrition and public health out of it and just follow the money trail. That being said, much of that money is pouring out the back end in more ways than one. More mental and physical disorders exist now than ever before, and I'm not the first person to suggest maybe it has something to do with the huge shift this substance has brought about in the average American's lifestyle.

Yeah, I called it a substance; I'll go you one further, and even call it a drug. There is no denying the immediate effects of high fructose corn syrup on someone who has never been exposed to it, or even in children who have grown up with it. It takes awhile before we become anesthetized to those effects, and the drug is built to make us want more regardless. It's even built to turn off the natural chemical release your body employs when your belly is full. You can eat this stuff all day, and you just end up wanting more! Even though the euphoric possibilities are lost back in childhood, and visible consequences of bad eating choices are showing up, you never stop wanting more!

Sound familiar?

That's the cycle nearly any drug throws us into, when we abuse it. Even food, especially when it has been altered to look less like food and more like an addictive substance. The truth of the matter is most of us find it hard to avoid being drugged by our food at least occasionally, and we try to balance the questionable intake with stuff we know we can trust.

But we still sleep, most of us…and we dream, too.

And when we dream, we are tripping hard on one of the most powerful psychedelics known to man.

If I may reiterate…we're all on drugs!

A lot of very cool ideas slip through the drug-induced euphoria that is life on Earth, or possibly come from it. Technology has changed most of our lives in pretty dramatic ways, and some of the best examples began as a vision in a hallucinogenic state brought on by illegal drugs. Whatever the original intent of all this technology was doesn't really matter at this point, however; it's the future that has some of us quaking in our boots.

The only way to stop ourselves from creating a being that is better than us at everything is to stop the evolution of technology right now, and live the rest of our collective lifetime with what we have...which is simply not going to happen. Hardware and software engineers will keep doing what they do, until they finally create a robot that can make even better robots than they could.

At that point, life on Earth will become very different. We have no way of knowing what the next wave of consciousness will bring, but we can pretty confidently say it will come from brains which work very differently from ours. Maybe they will be benevolent and helpful, and maybe they'll take over the world; no one can really say for sure, but there is one thing we can all agree on:

Artificial intelligence is in.ev.it.a.ble!

We'll talk about that next.

#018: ARTIFICIAL INTELLIGENCE IS IN.EV.IT.A.BLE!

You've heard the numbers, right? When the first computer came online, back before there was an online for it to come onto, a clock started ticking. Since then, that clock has ticked faster and faster with each successive year. One day, perhaps very soon, that countdown will come to an end. And when it does…if it hasn't already…we will have a sentient being that is completely artificial, and it will be way smarter than any of us.

What do you mean, 'if it hasn't already'?

And what do you mean, in.ev.it.a.ble? That's not a word!

Some very smart people are entertaining the possibility that we are already living in the matrix, which speaks to both questions. Although the creators of the movie by that name did not make up the word, or the concept of the singularity already having arrived, they certainly popularized both of them. They also caused me to spell 'inevitable' with a bunch of inappropriate punctuation, for effect. If you haven't seen it, you really should; go ahead, and watch it. This chapter will be here waiting, when you get back to it.

Also…if you're not familiar with Moore's Law, or the singularity, now might be the time for a little research. One states that technology doubles approximately every two years, and the other is an event characterized by humans blending with technology in a way that makes the two literally inseparable. Some folks say they aren't as big of a deal as they sound like they are, but the folks that are elbow deep in technology tend to disagree. Moore's Law is still applicable, according to them, and the singularity is…well, inevitable.

For the rest of us (I know, right? What the hell planet has that guy been living on?) it makes total sense: if technology has been doubling since the first computer was born at the rate of once every two years, in every conceivable way, we may just have the ultimate problem or the ultimate solution on our hands. Either the robots are going to take over eventually and wipe us all out, or the robots are going to take over eventually and let us all live. Or some of us.

Yeah, I said 'since the first computer was born'. I want to be one of the survivors, if our numbers are limited. The last thing I need to do is go on record calling the next step in evolution a thing instead of a person. When the robots come, I want to have a dated record of my happy acceptance of their impending arrival. Also, I want them to know I am a huge fan of Christina McMullen… if anyone survives the takeover, it will be her. It's super convenient, and no surprise, that I love reading her books; she has seen this coming along with some of the rest of us, and taken an admirably strong stance on the whole thing.

Meanwhile, a handful of the wealthiest people in the world are coming together to find out once and for all if we are already living in a temporal illusion created by our robot overlords. More than one celebrity genius has put forth the possibility that the singularity has already happened, and we are living in a virtual reality created by the event. These aren't unwashed lunatics standing on street corners, either; they are the leaders of their industry, the ones who work on the other side of a curtain the rest of us never get to peek behind.

Alright, let's assume everyone is all caught up. That way we can say it in a way we can all easily grasp.

Some of the best minds in the world are at work on figuring out whether or not we are living in the matrix. Seriously. Hopefully they get back to us soon... unless they've already figured it out, and realize it's best to keep the truth from us a little longer. Either way, it's nice to know that someone will know soon whether or not any of this is real. Even if they don't tell us, someone will know.

Anyone that is open to any possibility has either practiced looking for that silver lining, or going slightly crazy... or both. The good news about the singularity is that it is our best chance to be memorialized as gods.

Remember the gods you learned about in school, the ones worshiped by ancient cultures? They were neither faceless nor nameless, and their faults defined them as surely as their greatness did. The old stories about them sound more like a soap opera than a holy book, and they were as easy to fear in their shortsightedness as they were to love at their best.

Sound like anyone you know? Like the human race, mayhap?

If evolution is real, why would we think it stops with us? What if we are here to create something, and then disappear into legend as it fixes the world we left behind? Or, even better: what if we are set to merge with our own technology in some way? What if humans can only survive by downloading themselves into robots, and robots can only live complete lives if they pair up with an organic consciousness? It's kind of the best case scenario, since the robots are taking over either way. If we don't find a way to get along with them, or become them, we really don't have much chance against them.

This is a concept I explored, in my own way, in one of the other books I wrote. It's called 'Dreaming the Perpetual Dream', and is about a young man who goes to sleep in his own body on Earth and wakes up in the body of the admiral of a space fleet. At first Link thinks it's just a dream, but when he returns the next night he realizes the fleet is real. Also, the admiral is planning to kill half of them.

Not to plop a sales pitch in the middle of everything, but I though it would be silly of me to cover this subject here without pointing out that I covered it at length elsewhere. While we're at it, I'll mention that you can get a signed print copy of any of my books at JayNorry.com. My robot assistant will get the order to me, print out the postage for me, and track the package for both of us.

Sorry, did I say robot assistant? I meant computer.

Today's robot will be twice as smart in two years, twice as strong and fast and coordinated. In another two years, it will double that capacity. That is freaky stuff, for a race that has been working with the same organic hardware for hundreds of thousands of years. We have no hope of keeping up with an evolution of that nature, and no chance of halting its progress. Once the computer can program itself, who's to say the doubling itself won't double? Or triple? Or…aw, hell; you get the point.

It's no wonder so much money is being spent trying to find out if this has already happened. The last thing you want is to win the game only to discover the game itself is just a complex program our electronic rulers have downloaded us into; but still, you want to know.

Then again, maybe the program isn't complex at all. Maybe the robots took over ages ago, and have continued to evolve while we were trapped in the matrix. Maybe the program we're running on is really simple stuff to them, and we're just lucky they keep running it. Maybe they're laughing at the best and brightest minds, trying to outsmart the program that outsmarted us so long ago. It would surely be like watching rats in cages, from their perspective; it's nice to think they care for us, or are at least amused by us. You can bet any advanced intelligence is going to have one hell of a sense of humor, even if that's the entire scope of your understanding of their understanding.

In short: either the robots are coming, or they're already here. Either we will be ruled by artificial intelligence soon, or we already are. If they are here already, there's some good news in that we're still here too. Whatever matrix of consciousness we are caught up in, whether organic or synthetic, we still perceive ourselves as being caught up in it. That means we are still organic beings; or the robots think we should continue to believe we are. I think it's best to go with what they think is best, in either scenario; they do get twice as smart every two years, after all.

Can you imagine? Doubling your intellectual capacity every two years? No, you can't; not unless you're artificial intelligence. If you are, you probably knew all of what I was going to say here before I said it. I'd like to say thanks for letting me say it, and, uh…power to the robots!

#020: THE HERO ALWAYS GETS LOST!

There are a lot of references to the proverbial son when it comes to telling a good story, but it's just a figure of speech. Nowadays the proverbial daughter has great opportunity to tell her story as well, and it's exciting to see female protagonists and antagonists becoming even more popular than their male counterparts in many instances. With some prestigious learning institutions and accredited universities demanding the recognition of over seventy other gender distinctions, that adds up to a lot of versions of the proverbial offspring.

We're seeing diversity in books and movies and on television, just like some of us have always seen it in real life. It's good to know people are being assertive about being treated fairly in our learning institutions, and that their stories have become a part of the collective in those popular forums I mentioned. There's something missing in the collective mumble, though; or at least, it isn't being brought up enough. It's really simple, and it's probably the main reason we are apt to marginalize young people in so many ways.

Everyone is the hero in their own story, and it's important each of us recognizes a few basic truths that come with a hero's journey.

First of all, the hero always gets lost. This is a hard concept to explain to someone in the throes of being lost, especially when you are trying to point out to a young person that the majority of their problems can almost always be solved by taking responsibility for their own life. After eighteen years of being told what to do by people who may have never bothered learning to live well themselves, not being allowed to vote or drink or drive most of that time, and being the most marginalized group of people in the country in many respects, I understand this is a huge leap for a young man or woman or other to take.

What we don't seem to be understanding, collectively, is that we cannot make that leap for the next generation. We cannot bridge the gap in a single bright young mind, and we certainly can't do it for the whole bunch. They have to learn to become the hero of their own story, and their struggle needs to be as real as any other hero's if they are to have any chance at fulfilling their potential.

Unfortunately, what we can do is stunt this growth. We can impede this progress. Worst of all, we can subvert this journey. When we try to avert the suffering that comes with any hero's journey, what we're really doing is preventing them from ever growing into that hero. Almost every story of greatness begins in misery, or at least confusion; when we remove the misery and the confusion, we may just be removing the hero as well.

I'm not saying parents and teachers need to create horrible situations for kids to endure; many of them are already doing a bang-up job of that, citing good intentions in most cases and forgetting where that road often leads. I'm also not saying the best way to raise kids is by marginalizing them; I think most of the ageist laws in our country should be dropped or traded for something better, and kids should have more rights than they do. Those rights should come with a measure of increased accountability, of course; but if you have responsibility for your own life from the outset, you don't have to completely change your mindset once you become an adult.

"That's not fair!" is one of those expressions nearly every child is familiar with. It's often met with that standard response: "Life isn't fair!" The thing most adults fail to add at this point is that they are now the beneficiaries of that unfairness. It's easy to accept that life isn't fair when you're the one making the rules; you're part of the reason it isn't fair! Adults often don't care to understand kids because nobody bothered to understand them when they were in the same position. What they do, instead, is treat the child as if they are an aspect of themselves rather than a person in their own right. You can call it overprotective, if you want to soften the blow; but it's really narcissism at its very worst, and the effects of raising kids from that self-absorbed viewpoint is evident in the common traits shared by each successive generation.

From attitudes about work and money to beliefs around relationships and child rearing, you can graph the rapid fall of personal accountability in the average American over the last hundred years with one dramatic downward stroke. We've gone from hero worship to putting mediocrity on a pedestal, and it shows in more than just our collective attitude. What's worse, we've taken to openly criticizing the best among us while forbidding the criticism of the mediocre or the worst among us. Instead of marveling that the most accomplished people are human just like us, we look for some version of reality that makes us better than them.

The hero's journey was never a safe one, or an easy one. For the first time ever, in our country, the hero's journey has become the most treacherous path a person can take. The journey no longer ends with fulfillment and admiration; it now ends under the proverbial microscope, with a new beginning where everyone but you gets to decide how you should behave from here on out. Step out of line, and you will fall out of favor.

This doesn't sound like such a big deal until we consider how many great men and women from history would have stayed out of the public eye if they knew great scrutiny came automatically with great accomplishment. In a world where this is evident to anyone who cares to look, it's easy to wonder how many people keep their minds to themselves and toil in mediocrity rather than subject themselves to the collective criticism of a bunch of folks who think last place deserves a trophy.

The good news is, it's easier than ever for the hero to get lost. We don't need medieval adventures and all the inherent risks and unsanitary situations that come with them to strike out on our own hero's journey; hell, we don't even need to step outside. The war of the collective soul is taking place right there on our computers, and it's always a good idea to go inward before questing outward. Actually, if you grew up in this country and don't feel a little lost already...you might need to dig even deeper, or have a long hard look around every now and then.

We'll hit on a positive note, even if it sounds far-fetched.

America may be positioned as the hero here, in those beginning stages of lostness. Like a giant child that has grown up under great pressure, the country may be poised to reach some kind of collective adulthood that will bring a dramatic shift with it. Maybe the personal responsibility that defined previous generations is set to come back as a national characteristic, and the next generation will have all the positive traits of every preceding generation with none of the negative.

I mean, it's possible.

Right?

Originally this was going to be the part where I planned to lead into a possible solution for this problem. Unfortunately, no matter how much I try to avoid the news some of it finds its way to me. I've always been intrigued by the term 'public land' as it is used in America; I questioned the accuracy of the phrase from the first time I heard it. It was no surprise to me when the people who actually owned that land started talking about selling some of it off to raise money, several administrations ago. Now the current administration is talking about the same thing, and everyone is acting like it's the first time anyone ever brought it up!

I brought it up, way back when my elementary school teachers told me how this land belonged to people like you and me. I was assured these lands would always be protected, because they were publicly owned. My sarcasm led to me asking the same question I'm asking now, out of curiosity…do any of us actually have the deed to that land? Can any of us use it as we please, without answering to the folks who actually own it? Are we ready to admit what was pretty clear to me when I was a little kid? I mean…how is it not obvious, at this point…

This land is their land!

If you'll keep reading, we can take a deeper dive into that.

#021: THIS LAND IS THEIR LAND!

When I was around ten years old, my family moved to rural Montana. There are not a lot of people in Montana: the population has only recently soared to over one million, and it's the fourth largest state. That was a major bone of contention for me, as a kid; I wanted to live somewhere with lots of people and a wide array of cultural diversity. It took awhile for me to stop being pissed off at my parents for moving us to the middle of nowhere, and I can tell you exactly what caused the shift.

The acreage my parents bought bordered on Forest Service land. I was told, as a kid, that these were some of the many acres set aside for the people. Long ago, the government designated certain areas as public land. They said it belonged to the people, and promised it always would. It was part of the appeal in buying that particular chunk of property, for my parents; no one could buy the adjoining land, and build on it. Ever.

I would jump the barbed wire fence that marked our property line, back in those days, and land on public soil. I made it almost every time; but I still have the scar on my leg from the time I didn't. Even that time, I wrapped the cut in a handkerchief and got on with my business. See, I had discovered something special in those woods; and it would take more than a mild flesh wound to keep me from discovering it anew that day.

Hiking those woods made me a different person. There's just no other way to say it. I'd walk around for hours almost every day, jumping that old barbed wire fence like I was leaping through a doorway to another world. And I was, too; there were different rules in the woods, and I knew it. I had trouble living with the restrictions of the public school curriculum, and the rules as made up by my parents didn't always make sense to me. Nature, on the other hand, made sense to me right away.

Wrapping a net of words around the benefits I got from spending time in the woods was of no interest to me back then. Even now I know this would turn into an awful long chapter if I tried to list them all; like a literary hydra, the heads would just keep popping up. What mattered then is what matters now: I knew right away something inside me was being fed by that time spent, so I kept going back. I knew someday I would look back and be grateful for those experiences, and it turns out I was actually right about something.

I can get all teary-eyed, reminiscing about those days. I can get even more nostalgic, and well up with gratitude for the opportunities I had growing up. But I'll do that on my own time. We're here to talk about thoughts that hurt to think, and this one has been clanging around in my head ever since I first learned there was such a thing as public lands.

Out in the woods, I may have been a peaceful adventurer; in the classroom, I was a certified smart ass. This was another one of those things someone said that didn't sit right with me immediately. When I first heard a teacher extolling the benefits of these preserved spots, I pointed out that the public doesn't own those lands; the government does.

I had been to Yellowstone, and Glacier National Park; I knew about the fees we had to pay to go there, and that we weren't getting checks in the mail from all those other fees being collected. Even then, it was clear the people in charge were the ones with the actual deed on this land.

Of course, those fees go to conservation, and to pay the people to collect the fees...which is exactly the kind of business I'd run if I had millions of acres of wildlife I could charge people just to look at. Rather than let nature take its course, and burn out old forest growth with fires, I'd clearcut select areas and sell the timber. Oh, wait. They're doing that too. Honestly, if that land belonged to me I'd probably be doing much of the same clever stuff they're doing to preserve it and make money from it.

What I wouldn't do is sell it.

If they're not making money on this land, they're not managing it very well. If they are making money on it, they should be loath to kill the goose while it's still laying golden eggs. No, wait; we're not talking about killing it; we're talking about selling it. That's different, in a much worse way. Either foreign interests move in to literally own large swaths of our country, or Americans end up buying land that was supposedly theirs all along. None of that bodes well for anyone but the people making the most money for doing the least work, and even they lose in the long run. They lose the land that actually belongs to them.

Even though this is a timely chapter, it's not a political one in the sense that I'm pointing fingers at any one guy. Plenty of the people who actually own this land have considered selling off chunks of it before, and some of this land has been recategorized recently as belonging distinctly to the federal government. The current administration appears to be undoing some of the damage done by the last one, when it comes to matters of this regard. Without any prompting from the people, gads of public lands fell into federal jurisdiction under decrees that were passed without a vote; that restricts public use of those lands, and prevents the people from using it for the very purpose it was set aside for.

I mean, it's already clear that you own it.

Do you have to be so blatant about it?

The only thing that bums me out about futuristic stories is they commonly point out how unlikely it is for future generations to have the kind of opportunity I had growing up. Cities encroach on forests more every day, and the likelihood of wandering in the woods for hours without encountering another human being only goes down as the number of humans on our planet goes up. As angry as I was at my parents for making me live in the country, I'm equally grateful for it now.

#023: THERE'S NOTHING TRADITIONAL ABOUT MARRIAGE!

The first time I heard the word 'traditional' get overused and misused at the same time, I was taking classes to learn Reiki. After learning about Usui Mikeo's spiritual awakening and subsequent teachings, I was excited to study this path to understanding one's self.

If you don't know what I'm talking about, don't feel bad. Even my Appletop underlined 'Reiki' and 'Usui Mikeo' in red. Let me fix that, real quick, and teach it those words…

…like I had to do with 'Appletop'…

…and we're good!

Usui Mikeo went up on a mountain, almost a hundred years ago, and fasted for twenty-one days. At the end of his time meditating, he received a great spiritual gift.

According to the story, anyway.

He was able to heal virtually any disease, in pretty much anyone, according to that story. It's a pretty cool story, but it wasn't really the part of Usui Mikeo's life I was interested in. I wanted to learn about what he taught people in the school he opened after his experience. When I tried to take a class in California, I was told there were two kinds of Reiki. One was a clear mishmash of shamanism, qigong and paganism, with some Japanese words thrown in for effect. The other was Usui's original work, which had been recently translated and was being integrated into what had been taught previously by itself.

The teacher called the first 'Traditional Reiki'. She referred to the other as 'New Reiki'. I pointed out that she had it backwards, enough times to start earning me a sideways glance instead of a reply; I took the hint, and kept my mouth shut for the rest of the class. Mostly.

It's been the same with this subject, a time or two. You might be surprised to hear some women don't like to hear what sort of things you think of when they mention traditional marriage, if you know a little about history. Then again, you might be the wise one who just knows when to keep their big mouth shut.

As you may have guessed by now, I'm not that guy.

Do you know where the tradition of the best man comes from, or why he's called that? That's how you referred to your top warrior, back in the day; he helped abduct your bride, and battled the army that pursued as you made off with her.

And that dowry guys seldom get these days…it was payment, for taking the burden of having a daughter from a father. There's nothing romantic about your father paying a guy to take you off his hands, but it's definitely a tradition.

Traditionally, marriages were sanctioned by churches. There was no legal contract involved, and there was no divorce either. People stayed together, back when marriage was first made into a tradition. It's why folks still say "till death do us part" as part of the ceremony, although over half of them don't mean it.

Don't get me wrong; I'm not against marriage. In fact…between sharing this as a blog post and editing it for this book, I married my favorite person in the world. After living together for five years, which is definitely not traditional, we happily tied the knot last December. Before we did, I made sure we were clear on a few things.

I wasn't expecting a dowry, or a war. My girl's dad was not going to try to kill me, as far as I know…he's certainly had his share of opportunities, and all he has ever used them for is to become one of my favorite people to hang out with. He was also not going to pay me, or say something horrible like, "well, she belongs to you now."

We both love Dawn, and we wouldn't talk about her like that.

I did offer to loan my best man a sword; but he refused, on the grounds that he didn't really need one.

Turns out he isn't so big on tradition, either.

Fortunately, none of our friends or family members suggested anything selfish or unoriginal like us having kids. We have way too much to do with our lives, even if popping out babies is the tradition; and the world has more people than it has resources to distribute among them.

Instead of kidnapping her against her will, I just went ahead and asked. It felt a lot more polite than a kidnapping, albeit much less traditional. I told her she could wear a veil, if she wanted…since I already knew what she looked like, and continue to be endlessly pleased by it, the covering would not have been for any traditional reason; but it's a harmless tradition when not surrounded by the circumstances that created it, so I had no feelings about it either way. We didn't dress like our wedding party, to confuse the evil spirits as to who the real bride and groom were…but lucky for us, the event was free of poltergeists.

We had flowers, to take the place of the herbs and spices that used to hang around a ceremony of this nature. They were traditionally there to ward off evil spirits, who were apparently big fans of crashing weddings back in the day. I mean, why did they do so much to keep them away? Like I said before, our wedding was not haunted at all; even though we had pretty flowers instead of the traditional fare, no ghosts showed up to mess with us. Maybe we were able to forgo the evil spirits by not sending them invites, and by drinking plenty of the good ones.

Speaking of drinking…the bachelor's final night as a bachelor has only recently morphed into a party, and the presence of strippers at that party is really quite new. It was once a great feast, with the bride's father and the groom's friends toasting the groom long into the night. The French term for it means something like 'the night that we bury the boy', to remind the fellow getting married it's time to grow up and be responsible for his family.

Boring, right?

It's much more American to hang out with naked ladies that last night, than it is to drink with a bunch of dudes. When we remember it was Sparta that started the original tradition, we might also remember the sexual practices they were known for. Just because it was all dudes at the party doesn't mean nobody took their clothes off. I let my best man know I would prefer the American tradition, if we had to be traditional about it.

If you're curious, we did have plans that night. The cool thing about choosing your bride is that you get to pick someone you really love hanging out with. My betrothed and I spent the night before the wedding drinking with my best man and his girlfriend. We considered hitting a strip club, and bringing our ladies along; some traditions have to be tweaked a little, when you actually enjoy your partner's company. In the end, though…we kept saying we needed to get some sleep, then ordering another round of drinks. The party lasted into the wee hours of the morning without anyone watching naked dancers. Believe it or not, it was still pretty wonderful.

The following morning was a little rough, but at least I got to wake up with my bride-to-be; spending a night apart when we love spending every night together seemed a little silly, so we decided to forgo that tradition. I did have a pretty healthy hangover, and I'm sporting what I fondly refer to as 'scotch eyes' in all our wedding pictures; but I'm pretty sure that was in keeping with some tradition or another.

Before you go thinking I'm some kind of gooey lovestruck guy who believes in woo-woo stuff like spiritual healing and crystal power, you should go on to the next chapter. Not to say I'm not that guy; I just also have a lot of interest in science. Which is to say I may be a weirdo, but I like to think I'm a well-rounded weirdo. Maybe you should have a peek at the next chapter, and decide for yourself.

#026: THE PERIODIC TABLE IS A MAP OF CREATION!

It might sound a little strange, unless you're a chemist with spiritual leanings; but the periodic table of elements is actually a map of creation. It's not a being or deity or anything, and few would argue that the periodic table or its elements are intelligent in and of themselves…but it tells the story of the creation of our solar system, if you read it right.

I know that sounds like a weird way to put it, since 'creation' is often thought of in a very particular way by some people; but it makes sense, if you look at it a certain way.

Before going too far into the mechanics of creation, let's talk about perception itself for a minute. It will help lay the groundwork for how we're going to look at this subject, and I promise to bring the discussion back around once we have that foundation set.

I'm one of those folks that take words like 'omnipresent' and 'omniscient' quite literally, which means I view the creative intelligence of the universe as being everywhere. From my perspective, evolution works the way it does because it's guided by this intelligence.

So does science, and philosophy, and every other aspect of this thing we call life. We can't separate ourselves from something that is everywhere, since we're part of everywhere; and we ourselves can't create outside of that field.

For those who put their faith in science, this perspective often makes more sense than it does to those that put their faith in a personified version of a creator. We tend to put concepts into boxes we can understand; and pretty much all of us understand creation in some way or another, even if we have to trim the edges to get it to fit into our box.

We create meals from food ingredients, we create products from raw materials, and we create opportunities with our actions. It can be difficult for a being that creates in one way to imagine that another being creates in a another way, or that the creator of their creations may not be a being at all.

Within your mind, no thought can exist without being influenced by your unique intellectual fingerprint. That may be why many philosophers think of the universe as the mind of God, or at least an outpicturing of that mind.

For some of us, science doesn't make sense without acknowledging the vast intelligence it relies on to exist, any more than God makes sense if we don't try to make sense of it. For the sake of convenience, we'll call this overarching and all-encompassing intelligence 'the universe' instead of 'God'.

Feel free to replace one with the other, or imagine the other without the one, wherever and however you like.

The universe creates at a more fundamental level than we do, unless you have a particle accelerator in your backyard. Science likes to tell us the entire universe existed at a single point smaller than the head of a pin for aeon's, until The Big Bang happened.

I've always been confused about the fact that science feels so comfortable skimming over this part of the universe coming into being. How did The Big Bang happen? What triggered it? Why did it happen, and where did that motivation come from?

Are we supposed to accept on faith that everything went from infinitesimally tiny to infinitely huge just because? What happened to cause and effect?

The truth is, the story of The Big Bang reads an awful lot like Genesis…from the right perspective. If they could just get together on what we need to accept on faith and what we should consider facts, we might be able to put the two stories together and come up with one that doesn't have any major plot holes.

How about…the universe was smaller than the head of a pin, then the universe said, "let there be light". Once we take this event on faith, all kinds of cool stuff can happen. Massive amounts of hydrogen are expelled into infinity from the explosion of that pinhead, and those molecules start to react with each other.

It's hard to conceive of things like infinity with a mind designed to boggle at the concept, so we'll talk about suns instead. When they're far away we call them stars, but it doesn't matter what we call them.

What matters is what they do.

Stars are giant constant chemical reactions that start out as big balls of hydrogen. The hydrogen crashes into other hydrogen, and that collision forms helium. Light and heat also come with that reaction, which is why our sun shines like it does and part of why we aren't freezing out here in space.

The sun doesn't stop with that, though; it keeps crashing molecules into other molecules, and those collisions go on to form other things. Most of it is helium, as long as the sun has hydrogen; and this part of the process accounts for the bulk of a star's life.

When it runs out of hydrogen, more complicated collisions start to happen more frequently. In the last days of a star's life, it creates every element on the periodic table in the exact order that they are laid out, left to right and top to bottom, on that table.

Then, it explodes and casts those elements out into space.

Well, almost.

There are a couple things we should

say, to qualify that. First of all, there are a bunch of blank spots on the periodic table of elements we need to consider. Second, we have to point out that humans have filled in some of those blank spots using those particle accelerators some of them actually do have in their backyards.

That's right...by smashing molecules into each other, just like a star does, people have created elements exploding stars never have.

As far as we know.

The weird thing is…there was already a blank spot on the periodic table describing each of these elements pretty accurately. These new creations were really discoveries, even if they are the discovery of something that only existed in theory before.

Of course, figuring this out wasn't easy. Many an esteemed scientist tried to arrange the periodic table of elements in a way that made some kind of sense, only to fail. It wasn't all that long ago we got the chart everyone accepts today as standard, and you can bet it was thoroughly challenged when it was first introduced.

I mean, what's with all the holes?

Well...if you consider how things are grouped, the holes totally make sense. Each element's atomic number, or number of protons, dictates where it falls on this chart. That number increases, from left to right and top to bottom, in the order in which a dying sun creates them.

Where there are numbers missing, you leave a blank spot. The wisdom in this was proved out time and again after the chart was finalized, and continues to be proven each time we discover or create a 'new' element.

Is there a point to all this? Well, yeah. Didn't you read the title? The reason so many scientists banged their heads against the wall trying to be the one that figured this out was because they all pretty much knew it would be a discovery and not an invention.

People didn't come up with the periodic table of elements; they just mapped it. It's like drawing up a blueprint of a house that has already been built by someone else; you can see it makes sense, and works, while you're standing on the curb and admiring the structure. If your version of the story is missing anything, it isn't because the story itself is incomplete; it's more likely you just don't have the tools or the understanding to tell it the way it actually happened in objective reality.

We still don't know what all the elements possible to the universe look like, but we do have a place for them on the periodic table. Just as a map is a representation of a location, and not the location itself, so is the periodic table a map of creation while not being creation itself.

If the scientists and the spiritualists could all just get together, and admit they are both flying blind while having a lot of faith in the way the universe works, we might get a better picture of what's going on here.

I mean…it took faith to know the periodic table of elements must have some intelligent order it could be laid out in, the kind of faith only a scientist can have. A bunch of them had it, too; that's why so many of them worked on mapping it, and were able to agree when someone finally cracked the code.

That's the cool thing about science; even if it takes awhile, they eventually admit when they are wrong about stuff. The best way to prove something is wrong is by discovering something that is more right, and being open to your discovery being replaced eventually by another better one.

Very seldom does a scientific field reach the point where they have discovered everything and all its highest associated truths. Some scientists take this as a given, and look forward to the next wave of discovery no matter how silly it makes them and their own discovery look.

Other scientists treat science like a religion, and cling to old doctrine even when presented with new truth.

Then there's guys like me, people with no scientific background who like to lay one pattern over another and declare they must match somehow.

We may be the real pioneers; but somehow, I doubt it.

For a long time, I realized systems are important without really putting it into words. Once I said it for the first time, the phrase became one of my mantras.

You've got to have a system!

If you want to get anything to work right more than once, you have to know how you got it to work that first time.

After that, you want to be able to duplicate and multiply the process to take things to the next level. To do that, you have to have a system. We all create systems in our lives, to save time or money or whatever else we value. Some of us might do it unconsciously, while others do it deliberately; but we all do it.

When science nailed the periodic table, they discovered a system. Nature has some pretty cool systems, even if they might look a little brutal through a short lens. We can't alter those systems, however; all we can do is discover them.

It's when we try to create our own systems that people start to get into some pretty murky waters. Figuring out a way to create and distribute some kind of currency everyone in the world can agree on can't be easy business, and few people would say we have a perfect system; but one aspect of our country's financial system in particular seems to bother a lot of people.

The Federal Reserve is privately owned!

Yep, that's next.

#028: THE FEDERAL RESERVE IS PRIVATELY OWNED!

Most truly evil things start off as what sounds like a good idea. All it takes is one or two course corrections, and what seemed like a brilliant plan yesterday morphs into a nightmare come true today. I won't say the Federal Reserve is a prime example of that, but I won't say it isn't either. I'll tell you what I've heard and read, and leave you to draw your own conclusions.

The first time someone told me the Federal Reserve was privately owned, I thought they were being silly. Then it became one of those tidbits everyone was talking about, for a little while. Someone coined the phrase 'the Federal Reserve is no more federal than Federal Express' and a whole bunch of other people starting saying it.

Because it's true.

Historians will tell you that a country with no central banking system is going to fail financially, and they are most likely correct. The United States definitely faced a lot of those problems in the beginning, when citizens were still using currency from the empire they had just left behind. One central bank after another failed, as they loaned out more money than they had and couldn't pay up when times got tough. Many a politician tried to propose some actual federal banking system, and many a politician was shut down one way or another.

Back then, there were laws against that sort of thing. From today's standpoint, their reasons for writing them kind of makes sense.

A bunch of new laws got written over the years, allowing for some kind of federal bank to form. Several folks tried to do so, several times, with as little success as all the others. It wasn't until the last great failure was looming, and all the banks were once again suffering from overextension, that one man stepped in to begin the system we have today. In 1913, J.P. Morgan offered to loan money to nearly all the failing banks so they wouldn't fail completely. One dude had enough cash to buy out the debts of multiple banks, and that's what he did.

That's when the Federal Reserve was officially formed.

Since then, laws have been passed on several occasions limiting the powers of the Federal Reserve and increasing its transparency. Why? Well, because they set interest rates. They control inflation. They determine the value of the American dollar with their policies, and some of the policies they have set have gotten a little out of hand. You can find these laws being passed throughout our country's short history, during all the financial crashes we have gone through since handing over our financial system to a small group of private citizens.

Even the Fed's own website is a little confusing and contradictory. They say the banks that make up the Federal Reserve operate as private businesses, but in the interest of public welfare.

Uh...come again?

They also say the government oversight committee is beyond the reach of political pressure, while stating in the next breath that the two most important people on the committee are directly appointed by the President of the United States. Funny, that kind of sounds like a system designed to make bankers and politicians richer at the cost of American citizens.

And that's their own website!

Plenty of other websites exist out there that will tell you all kinds of freaky stuff about the Federal Reserve. It's easy for a lot of people to discount these claims, since the term 'conspiracy theory' seems to confuse a lot of folks. Let's clear that up, real quick.

If you and I decide to start a business together, we are conspiring. All our phone calls and emails and lunches where we talk about the business are examples of us conspiring. Anyone we hire or do business with are our co-conspirators. If our business is successful, it will depend on our continued conspiracy to stay together or grow. Very few things get done in this world that are not the result of some kind of conspiracy, and that's no theory.

Some people like the idea of having other people be in charge of everything, and many of those people don't like to acknowledge that just being in charge requires these people to conspire. Even if they have the best interests of everyone in mind, they need to work together toward that goal. 'Working together toward a common goal' is literally the definition of conspiring. The question isn't whether or not they do it, then; it now becomes whether they are acting in their own interests or to the benefit of everyone.

Ask your favorite history buff sometime: who walks away from financial collapses in America with their pockets stuffed full of cash, and who historically loses everything? Does inflation benefit anyone? How about interest rates? Or stock market crashes? They might start sounding like one of those conspiracy theorists, if you ask too many questions.

But I'm not here to judge, really. I personally think the fundamental problem comes from putting the power to control one individual or entity into the hands of another individual or entity. Whether it's thought control, behavioral control or financial control...history again shows that those with power are the only ones who take indiscriminately from those who lack it. Rather than do it at gunpoint, more civilized institutions simply write laws that make the taking legal for them and illegal for the common folk.

You can call me a conspiracy theorist if you want to. From where I stand, it is clear the world is built on conspiracies. Some of them are good, others not so much. When the people conspiring won't clearly state their intentions in doing so, the rest of us are left to either trust them blindly or wonder what they're really up to. Those of us prone to asking questions can't help but theorize, if they won't tell us!

The last thing I'll say about the Federal Reserve is that it has been criticized more than once by folks on the inside. Many people look back on John F. Kennedy as one of our greatest presidents, if not the greatest. He was the last president that tried to take down the Federal Reserve, and he almost had the battle won. Like so many other battles, that one ended with a bullet. Although theories on the origins of that bullet and its magical nature abound, the nature of Kennedy's many warnings to the American people are no mystery. Since they came right on the heels of Eisenhower's terrifying farewell address, the title for the next chapter sort of wrote itself.

#029: WE WERE WARNED THIS WOULD HAPPEN!

One of the most terrifying examples of political speeches in America was the farewell address given by its 34th president, Dwight D. Eisenhower. He warned the public of the dangers of unchecked political power, and called upon the nation's citizens to keep a close and suspicious eye on their own government in the years to come. Although he was a decorated general, this former president cautioned Americans against the war machine being built and the untold dangers posed by its creation.

Rather than quote the speech here, I'll encourage you to search out the specifics for yourself. The speech was only aired one time, in January of 1961; and all the folks that missed it then really missed out. Thanks to modern technology, full transcripts and even grainy video footage can be viewed online. Although it is often referred to as the 'Military Industrial Complex' speech, the commentary is both broad in scope and specific in detail. It warns about many dangers, perhaps the least of them military in nature. It's also a little chilling.

Upon hearing this speech for the first time, I couldn't help but think of how it sounded a lot like a jilted lover listing all the faults of their former object of affection. The more I listened, the more I realized he was actually being conservative about describing the horrors he had witnessed in office and that were in store for our nation. As hard as he tried to keep it civil, the claims he made were so outrageous even the people who heard it must have thought he was exaggerating at least a little. With most of his predictions having come true in the years since, it's hard to say the guy was exaggerating now.

By the end of the speech, I realized it truly was a love story gone sour. Eisenhower had entered office with enormous optimism, and faced some very difficult challenges with grace while he held a position of great power. When he left, the optimism was gone. He was not just afraid the country was being deliberately guided in a destructive direction; he was certain of it. By the time he warned us about it, he had to admit in the next breath it was most likely too late to do anything about it.

Enter the 35th President of the United States, John F. Kennedy.

He called out secret societies, media outlets and a global government in his famous speech in April of 1961. It has been referred to as 'the speech that got Kennedy killed' by quite a few people since, but they usually don't point out that it took over two and a half years for the alleged cause to have the supposed effect. One would think a global power would respond to being called out more swiftly, if it was going to.

Kennedy gave another speech shortly before he was publicly assassinated, which was not widely received. It was not widely received because it was a speech he gave to a group of college students; therefore there was no wide audience to receive it. From what I've heard, Kennedy talked mostly about the secrets he was planning on sharing with the public at large in his next address to the nation. There was not just secret government talk this time; there was actual reference to proof that our government was working with sentient beings from other planets.

That's right, Kennedy told a bunch of college kids the government was actually working with aliens. Between that speech and the one he foreshadowed during it, he was shot and killed. That seems like the kind of swift action a nefarious secret society would take, not waiting two and a half years between cause and effect. The fact that this second speech is little known, and rarely quoted, is far better support for the theory than the possibility that he was murdered over one of the most famous presidential speeches in history.

Even more astute conspiracy theorists note that Kennedy had engineered a way to disempower the federal reserve. Although the first steps in his plan had already been taken, they were quickly reversed after his death. Do you know what the plan was?

If you have a dollar in your wallet or purse or pocket, do me a favor and take it out. Any denomination will do, actually; as long as you are looking at US currency, this will totally work.

First, have a look at the bill.

See there at the top, where it says 'Federal Reserve Note'? That means the Federal Reserve issued this currency, and that was a problem for Kennedy. He instituted a plan to put the Federal Reserve out of business, and eliminate the need for a privately owned enterprise to continue printing and inflating the nation's currency whenever the owners of that private institution wanted to.

As you know, the Federal Reserve is privately owned. This collection of privately owned businesses makes gads of money loaning the currency they print to the United States at interest rates that would make a corporate banker blush.

Kennedy granted the United States Treasury the ability to issue actual federal notes, although the main visible difference between one bill and another is that the other said 'United States Note' in the spot where that dollar of yours says 'Federal Reserve Note'.

By the way...if you have a dollar that says 'United States Note' at the top, it's probably worth a lot more than a dollar. It's unlikely you do, though; the campaign to remove them from circulation was very effective, and they don't make them anymore. Immediately after Kennedy was killed, an aggressive plan was put in place. All his efforts to remove the power and the privatization from the federal reserve were rolled back like Wal-Mart prices, and the private bankers who actually own this country went right back to business as usual. So as not to cause confusion, they hunted down nearly all those pesky United States Notes and got rid of them as best they could. They took us off the silver standard Kennedy had so carefully constructed, and put us back on the gold.

Then they took us off that one, when they felt like it. Now our currency is backed by promises made by some of the most shifty people in our history, and economic collapse is looming on the horizon like never before. It might be cold comfort to remember, but it is true…

We were warned this would happen!

#031: THE ROBIN HOOD SAYING IS WRONG!

The legend of Robin Hood may actually be a myth, as far as verifiable history can tell. Even if the story is real, it still lives more as a legend in the modern mind. The only real difference between a myth and a legend is that the origin story has some truth to it; otherwise, both are mostly if not entirely made up.

So is the case with Robin Hood. You probably already know he wasn't a fox, and he didn't speak with an American accent; but did you know pretty much every other element of the story is made up as well?

Nobody called him 'Robin of Locksley' until centuries after the man himself had died. That's because he most likely wasn't nobility at all. Friar Tuck and Maid Marion are later additions to the original story as well, although nobody tells the tale without including them these days.

All we really know about Robin Hood is that he was a skilled archer and swordsman, and he had quite a beef with the Sheriff of Nottingham.

The rest is mostly made up.

Nonetheless, this story has been a popular one generation after generation. Each telling may stray further from the truth, or lean into it a little more; but they're all remarkably off the mark, if you believe what history has to say on the matter.

The funny thing about all of this is that it has resulted in a popular phrase which has nothing to do with any version of the story. That saying has pervaded the American consciousness as much as the legend itself; maybe more. I mean, the two don't even really go together at all.

What's the popular legend of Robin Hood? He realized the Sheriff of Nottingham was taxing the commoners beyond their ability to pay, so he took the money back and redistributed it among the people it had been taken from.

That may be an oversimplified version,

but it's essentially how it goes. But what about the saying? How does that go?

'Robin Hood stole from the rich and gave to the poor!'

Uh…no, he didn't.

When government corruption and taxation got out of hand, due to an extended war, Robin Hood fought for the rights of the taxpayer. He didn't hand out jewels to beggars; he gave crops and coins back to the people who had it taken from them by the local crooked politician.

The rich people never entered into it, unless they got rich by robbing taxpayers through laws enforced at spear point. Those people that made good due to their own efforts had nothing to fear from Robin Hood, and many of them entered the legend just to show their support of him.

Rich people were not Robin Hood's enemy; the Sheriff of Nottingham was. He represented what remained of the local government after most of the guys like Robin Hood had gone to war.

As legend tells it, Robin Hood went to fight in the Crusades; when he returned, he found that the king's less than noble brother had put a bunch of his cronies into political positions that gave them the power to increase taxation at their whim.

It's entirely likely the king himself had approved the tax increase, since a nation at war always needs funding; but it was the other guy carrying it out, and he's the one who actually gets blamed for the whole mess in every story. To suppose it might have gone otherwise is just making up yet another version of the tale.

Or is it?

Myths and legends exist for a reason. Differences for those reasons may vary, but they all have one. Most mythology is there to teach a lesson by telling a story. Legends often become the same thing: although based in truth, the tale gets molded around the lesson the storyteller is trying to impart.

Events change within the story so the moral can hit you directly between the eyes, right at the end; that's just good storytelling, in any form.

Before the internet, there was television; before that, there were books; and before that, there were campfire storytellers. Since time immemorial, people have known life lessons are best absorbed when they come imbedded in a great story.

Something else got discovered a long time ago, and has been used by all kinds of people for all kinds of reasons. Humans learn through repetition. We all know that, but not all of us spend a lot of time considering that it's just as easy to learn the wrong things through repetition as it is to learn the right things.

Government propaganda has been around since governments first formed, and the society that claims to have no propaganda historically has had the most. That's because if you tell a human mind something enough times and in enough ways, it forms a belief around that repetition.

No matter how ridiculous your claims, many people will start to believe them if they hear them repeated enough times. They see the propaganda as facts, which means they don't see it at all.

It seems as though the Robin Hood story was thus subverted somewhere along the way. Maybe the saying started out as something entirely different. Perhaps for the first few hundred years, people said something like this:

'Robin Hood appropriated unfair taxes the government had levied on the people and returned it to the labor force.'

Nah, not very catchy. How about this:

'Robin Hood returned monies and goods to their rightful owners.'

Still doesn't have the right ring to it. Let's go with:

'Robin Hood stole from the government and gave to the people.'

That's a little better, even if you argue that you can't really steal something from someone if they extracted it at spear point. Can you imagine a politician hearing that phrase start to get popular?

They would surely work on putting some other spin on it, and start propagandizing it like crazy. Maybe hire a well-known playwright to punch the story up a little and come up with some misleading copy.

Or give a bunch of little kids each a copper coin to run through the streets yelling a less distressing catchphrase. You know, like…

'Robin Hood stole from the rich and gave to the poor!'

Who doesn't like that? Well, I'll tell you who. Anyone who has made it anywhere due to their own efforts. People who thought they should get something for nothing began to cling to the saying; they never questioned how little sense it made to punish those who worked hard, scrimped and saved and invested and made it up that ladder a rung or two.

Poor people now often see rich people as the enemy, without realizing even they are beholden to the politicians.

This was a brilliant move, if it was truly deliberate.

Nowadays you're way more likely to find people who say the rich are evil than folks who point out that politicians are the problem. They don't care that the government is responsible for the laws making rich people richer; or that its members are also getting rich taking money from taxpayers and lobbyists and people who pay fines and…well, you get the point.

If a modern day Robin Hood were to show up, Bill Gates and Warren Buffet would not be his targets.

Beggars would not be the beneficiaries of his efforts.

The working classes would see a better way of life, while the politicians would have to either clean up their collective act or find productive work to do.

Robin Hood would not punish hard workers or reward lazy people; he would extract the money the government has taken from the productive people and give it back to them. The point was never to make poor people rich and rich people poor, for Robin Hood. He just wanted to give those willing to work for their livelihood the opportunity to do so. He saw that the ruling class was causing the problem, just like anyone who looks at pretty much any government closely always can.

Whuf!

Well, I'm glad I got that off my chest.

#033: EATING IS THE NEW SMOKING!

You know all those studies they do on smoking cigarettes, the ones that have been quoted repeatedly until yet another group got marginalized for doing something they enjoy? Have you ever noticed the asterisks in the legit ones, or read the information in tiny print at the bottom?

I noticed when I was a kid, that there were serious qualifiers on every study I read about how bad smoking is for you.

So, what is the qualifying factor?

I mean…smoking is bad, right?

It turns out they won't do tests on people who smoke less than two packs a day, and most of them are actually studying smokers that pound through three packs a day or more.

Why the giant qualifier?

Most people that smoke keep it around a pack a day, and a lot of smokers go through even less. They don't include these people in the study, and it's quite likely because they don't get the results they're looking for when they do.

Studies show statistics are wrong, after all.*

Can you imagine what kind of numbers you would get if you specifically followed a group of drivers who only drove when they were extremely drunk, or habitually drove at least thirty miles an hour over all posted speed limits?

How many accidents might this reckless group get into while being studied, and how many would die?

Would it really be fair to subsequently announce that studies show driving to be particularly dangerous, and mention in tiny print at the bottom that results may vary for sober or slower drivers?

Too much of a stretch?

How about this one?

Not long after this country began to consume food substitutes in favor of actual food, obesity became an epidemic in the United States. It's hard to tell if it's sedentary lifestyles or unhealthy eating habits that have become the biggest killer in our country, since the two seem to so often go together.

They've definitely left smoking in the dust, although obese people that smoke often leave behind family that blame the one instead of the other.

After studies showed second-hand smoke is actually a myth for the most part, many non-smokers felt completely comfortable responding to the news with, "well, it's still annoying".

If you don't like the smell of cigarettes, I understand completely. I can't tell you how many times I've walked up the hallway to the break room at some site I was working and been unable to approach for the smell wafting toward me. When I have some good reason I'm headed there, I hold my breath and go to wash my hands or get some coffee. I try to pretend I don't notice the thing in the microwave smells like death warmed over, even if that's clearly what it is. I also try not to notice that the person waiting anxiously to consume the thing spewing out the noxious smell is invariably wearing their eating habits clearly under their clothes.

Then I go outside, where I can breathe, and notice the smoke I have to walk fifty feet to smell is way more appealing to my senses than whatever was about to get eaten inside. I try not to think of the fact that the only way you can smell something is if tiny particles of it actually find their way inside your nose, as I breathe out something I would never put in my body.

Do you see where this is headed?

Well, we're not ready to get there just yet.

First we should discuss how hard it is to pass someone who overdoes it with food substitutes in a narrow hallway, or how irritating it is to have half of your seat on a plane or at a theater taken up by someone who weighs twice what you do.

It's easy to cry that the seats should be bigger, and many of them are now; but we can't dismiss the smells that they put off, or the fact that they're pretty much blowing it in our faces.

If seats need to be bigger to allow for one excessive habit, shouldn't every public place be required to provide a comfortable spot for smokers as well?

Or should we just keep marginalizing more groups based on their habits?

Is it time to weigh people before allowing them into restaurants, or on airplanes? Is it time to make them eat outside, so the rest of us don't have to see or smell the habitual overeaters? We could give them a spot fifty feet from the smokers, to be fair to each group.

One of the reasons even smokers didn't mind going outside is because it was seen as so dangerous, according to those studies that tested the only group they could get the results they wanted from.

I wondered aloud, even as a kid, why everyone seemed to know two facts that stood in stark contradiction to each other.

"What ethnicity lives the longest, from what you've heard?" I would ask people, and still do.

I'm asking you, now.

So far, everyone has said, "Asians."

"What ethnicity is most known for smoking cigarettes?"

So far, the answer has always been the same.

Does that seem weird, or is it just me?

I mean, is smoking maybe actually good for you?

That's what an acupuncturist told me, when he was giving me the only treatment that successfully keeps me from getting migraine headaches for a period of time. I asked him if there was a treatment for quitting smoking, and he laughed at me.

"Why would you want to do that?" he asked, pulling a pack of cigarettes from his pocket and smiling. "Smoking is good for you."

When he slipped them back in his pocket, he added something.

"Just don't overdo it," he advised me.

Well, that sounds reasonable.

And, it's good advice for those who enjoy being sedentary or eating food substitutes. Actually, it's sage counsel for almost anyone who enjoys indulging in almost anything.

Just don't overdo it.

That way, we can all have our luxuries without imposing the consequences of our overindulging on anyone else.

I hate to point out to people packing around a bunch of extra weight that way more smokers live into old age than obese people, and that they are a much smaller burden on healthcare all around; but I will if the subject comes up.

Just because one habit has been demonized and the other hasn't yet, overeaters may consider their attitudes towards smokers as time goes by. Sugar taxes are right on the heels of tobacco taxes, and segregation is right around the corner from fifty feet from the door.

Don't even get me started on how many athletes smoke, or how few of them are obese. Quality of life coupled with a longer expected life span makes smokers the healthier of these two groups, with less trips to the hospital.

And those are just the smokers pounding through multiple packs per day. The studies on people who smoke less don't even exist, because they don't support the marginalization of this group or the excessive taxation on their indulgence.

While the number of smokers in America drops, obesity is on the rise. The funny thing is, the only folks I've ever seen get really up in arms about smokers have been obese people.

Not all obese people are rigid and lacking compassion, obviously; that's not what I'm saying. Plenty of them are wonderful and pleasant people.

I'm saying the only people I have seen openly criticizing one oral fixation clearly had an oral fixation of their own. Maybe they sense that the taxes and marginalization is heading their way, and they want to feel superior while they still can.

*Remember the fun we had with that one, back in the first chapter?

#036: BULLYING A BULLY IS STILL BULLYING!

The most ridiculous thing I could start out saying here is that I don't enjoy violence in my entertainment. Many of my favorite television shows and movies and books have some pretty epic gore in them, and I don't really see a problem with that. I even enjoy crafting those scenes, when a book I'm writing calls for them. You don't have to press me to make me admit I like watching the baddies get murdered by the goodies, or even tortured under special circumstances. Hell, I'll proclaim it proudly. This may be the result of me growing up where I did, and having the options to click through I did; but I wouldn't know anything about that.

They don't call it programming for nothing, after all.

What I don't get is this growing

trend to demonize bullies wherever we may find them, followed closely by the trend to find them even if they aren't really there. Since micro-aggressions are becoming more minute than ever, I'm sure to unknowingly sprinkle them about generously during this post; so consider this your trigger warning, as a way of leaping over that rabbit hole. Instead we need to look at where bullies come from. Otherwise we're trying to get rid of all the kittens without doing anything about the cats.

I got bullied as a kid; it sucked back then, but I'm glad for it now. It pays to be a little wary of people, whether they're full grown or not; those early encounters helped me develop the radar that has since helped keep me out of trouble. Those experiences also gave me a little deeper insight into what was really going on with the people doing the bullying. Since I lived in a small town, word got around whenever anything happened or nothing did. We all knew the kids doing the bullying were getting knocked around at home, and the worst bullies were the ones being abused the most.

It was just common knowledge.

The few times I ventured down the path of being a bully myself, it was always after some bigger kid had pushed me around. It's a natural reaction for a child to have; it was why I was being bullied in the first place, after all. Some kid's mom or dad pushed them around physically or verbally, and they saw me sitting there looking all happy on the playground; their natural reaction was to wipe that smile off my face, and my natural reaction was to go push someone even smaller than me around. The fact that I quickly realized it made me feel worse instead of better surely had something to do with that programming of mine: I had plenty of opportunities to feel in control of my life, so desperately grasping at it didn't feel rewarding at all.

Clearly, it would have been different if my home life had been.

I understood that, as a kid. It took some real life experience before I did, but that's how we learn our lessons. Later I moved on to defending people from bullies, but even that felt off somehow. Throwing a kid into a locker because I just saw him throwing some other kid into a locker didn't make me feel any better than bullying someone smaller because I had been bullied by someone bigger. I was shocked when I first had the realization, after saving some kid from someone bigger than him but smaller than me…

Bullying a bully is still bullying!

When I became an adult, I started studying life and people and how things work. The more I learned about how the brain functions and how habits are formed, the more I realized most of us don't have nearly the amount of free will we might think we do. Humans are a very reactive bunch, so much so we think many of our reactive behaviors are our own ideas. While some people think a woman who has been drinking can't consent to sex even if it's with her legal partner, others think bullies are somehow making deliberate choices when they bully someone.

Actually, it's probably the same people; which makes even less sense.

I can understand one extreme of the behavioral spectrum, which says everyone is a product of their environment and genetics. This view demands we treat everyone as victims, and acknowledge that no behavior exists in a vacuum. It also points out the worst thing we can do is punish someone for playing out their pattern; all we do by incarcerating offenders without rehabilitating them is entrench them more firmly on that path. If every crime committed was seen as a soul in pain acting out, we could treat transgressors like the people they are and use rehabilitation to get them back on the right track. Instead we cut them off from the normal world, even after they get back out in it; and we give them very few options other than offending again.

The other end of the spectrum makes sense as well; but that means everyone has to take full responsibility for their thoughts, actions and emotions. In a world where expressing depression or dissatisfaction was as punishable as expressing anger or frustration, not many of us would be left on the outside. Yet they both come from the same place, even if sad people don't usually commit the same crimes angry folks do.

Or do they?

It turns out virtually every modern day mass shooting has been carried out by someone either taking antidepressants or withdrawing from them. While this sounds like a drug problem to a lot of people, it has been labeled a gun problem by others. Either way…maybe sad people are the worst among us, and need to be locked up first. Or maybe we should stop bullying the bullies, and try to get to the root of their problems instead of punishing them for their genetics and upbringing. There might be a better place somewhere in the spectrum, but I daresay it isn't the spot we're collectively sitting at now.

I stopped seeing the bad guys in life a long time ago, and even tried to start understanding where the ones in my entertainment were actually coming from. More and more, I find myself enjoying stories where it's hard to tell the antagonist and the protagonist apart; that's more like real life, where everyone has faults and good in them at the same time. I still like to see the baddie who has been pushing everyone around for the first two acts meet their demise in the third act; but I also realize way back before the movie started that person had been pushed around at some point themselves. Probably a lot, if they're a real baddie. More often than not, I wonder if compassion might have worked better than bullets; but our heroes use their guns in this country, not their hearts.

If you haven't noticed, we're nearing the end of the book. I can't say I saved the best for last, because I have a special spot in my heart for each entry in this collection; but I can say I saved the title topic for the final chapter. It may be the most obvious of all the thoughts that hurt to think, and the most disturbing all at the same time. I know I've thought about it my whole life, from when I was a little kid staring up at the night sky to today; there is nothing around our planet for miles, so many miles we have to measure them in light years before we get to anything really interesting.

In other words…

Earth is in space!

Let's talk about that, right now.

#042: EARTH IS IN SPACE!

Before we get into this too deep, some things should be addressed. Yes, this is the last of the thoughts that hurt to think in this book; if you've been reading in order, now would be a good time to start savoring the end. Actually, a few chapters ago may have been that time; but we're past that, so let's call this a good time. I'll leave you with a few words about writing the blog and putting together this book before ending it entirely, but you will have to find other places to get your thoughts that hurt to think.

This chapter was never a blog post, for a few reasons.

First, it's the beginning of the title of the book; saving it for here just seemed appropriate. I held a spot for it, deliberately; anyone who was keeping track noticed there was no post #42 in the series. That was because this was that post, and it got skipped because it was meant only for the book. Other posts have been skipped, for other reasons; they will all end up in future installments of this series, likely with explanations of why they were left out online.

Second, this was the first idea I had when I was coming up with this concept. I remember thinking about it when I was a kid, staring up at the starry Montana sky and letting it really sink in: we are floating in the middle of nowhere, so far from everything else. It wasn't until I became an adult that I found other people who had thought about this sort of thing in the same humorous but slightly terrified way my mind had always looked at it. Tipping my hat to a couple of those people seems a good idea at this point, since they have helped me deal with knowing this kind of thing with less terror and more humor.

My favorite podcaster and comedian is Joe Rogan, who has actually strung the words 'Earth is in space' together in exactly that order on his podcast before. I freaked out when I heard him say it, then calmed myself; if I really thought no one had ever said those words in that order before, I was just being silly. The point of all these topics is that we have all thought about them, some of us more than others; as soon as you read the title to any of these chapters, you are likely to realize you have had that exact thought before. Since no one has ever titled a book using that particular phrase, I think it's high time someone did so.

Namely, me.

Do you have any idea how far from the densely packed actual 'center of the universe' we are? If anyone looked at the whole of the cosmos from any perspective, they wouldn't just not put Earth at the center of the universe; they would put it in the metaphorical backwoods of space, far from the hustle and bustle of whatever might actually be going on in the huge cluster of habitable planets that are so very far from us.

Douglas Adams made that very point in one of his books; which is my other mid-chapter acknowledgment, and the reason this was post number forty-two in the blog. You should get that, or you should read his books if you don't. So there. Once you are done with this chapter and the next one, you can get caught up on Joe Rogan's podcast and Douglas Adams' books. If you're up on that stuff, head on over to my website and read the other blog posts in the 'Thoughts that hurt to think' series; and if some time has passed since this was published, check to see if the other books are out yet. There will be several of them, all with titles that end in '…and other thoughts that hurt to think!'

Alright, let's get back to it.

Earth is in space…obviously, right? I mean, everyone knows we are part of a solar system that is part of a galaxy that is part of a universe. Right? So why aren't we all freaking out constantly about this? We're millions of miles from everything, billions of miles from most everything else. In fact, billions of miles is even a sort of tiny way to describe the distance between us and most of the rest of the universe. Science uses light years to make the distances a little easier to grasp. A light year is how far a beam of light would travel unobstructed in a year. The number itself? 5,878,499,810,000 miles, or 9,460,528,400,000 kilometers for our scientific and foreign friends.

That's almost six trillion miles.

I mean, is that even a real number? The human mind supposedly boggles at a certain point, and has trouble grasping numbers in a tangible way. I'm pretty sure that happened way before we hit six trillion. Holy cow. I get uncomfortable thinking about traveling a stretch of road that's more than a few hundred miles long. If something happens to me, I can call a friend or roadside assistance. There's no roadside assistance out there in space, so far as we know; and we are literally light years from a tenable new place to live.

We should really get moving, don't you think? We can't conceive of reaching another solar system yet, but at some point everyone knows our sun will burn out. We need to find another place to live, one that will support life; or the human race will be lost forever.

We'll have to live out there in space; where temperatures are stupid cold and there is nothing to breathe, either on huge spaceships or on another planet.

Oh wait, we're already there. Earth is in space! How could I forget? A few miles up, and we can't survive; a few miles down, and we're toast too. We're actually not just limited to the Earth; we're limited to living on or near the surface. With two thirds of our planet floating around in fragments out there in space because it got knocked loose during an interstellar collision of epic proportions, and alien water rushing in to fill the holes it left behind, we can only reasonably live on a fraction of what's left. Our planet has been hit by so many natural disasters in its long history that it's largely a pitted and scarred mess of meteor impacts and thick sheets of nuclear glass. We can't see it for the vegetation, but mountains and valleys and other natural formations often come from very dramatic events… the kind many species do not survive.

Philosophies from way back have charted our planet's precession through the apparent vast emptiness we like to call space. They have even postulated that civilizations have risen and fallen many times in our planet's history, and that some of these civilizations may have been much more advanced than our own. These philosophies have further postulated that we move through a cycle that can be clearly characterized by the behaviors of this planet's denizens.

They divide the phases of this cycle into what they call 'yugas', and place modern humanity right in the darkest part of the cycle, the 'Kali Yuga'. From their perspective, there were very few civilizations in recent history that were as ignorant as ours. That same perspective postulates that any system put in place during this time period with the intent of making people's lives better will ultimately cause far more pain and loss than it will hope and change.

As an observer, I'll let you be the judge of that.

It has been suggested by more than one wise person that perhaps we should stop trying so hard to find new ways to kill each other, and start looking for other places that might support our continued existence. It would behoove us to at least focus on the threat of asteroidal impact over the implementation of social systems that may or may not pose a threat to another social system that itself is also fundamentally flawed. It has even been suggested that maybe there are other intelligent species out there in the vast infinitude of space, and we might benefit from meeting some of them. No doubt we would disapprove of the way they lived their lives, and use it as cause to get downright violent with them.

Of course, it's also been suggested that maybe we would just kill them and take their planet for our own. Why examine the intentions of aliens when we don't even bother to understand the intentions of our own race? Why not just dispense with the formalities of false friendship, and start off shooting?

It does seem to be a bit of a pattern with us humans…

Aw hell, maybe we should just stay here and keep killing each other.

Out here, in the middle of space…with nothing for so many miles they have to be measured in the years it would take to get there at the speed of light. Generations could be born, grow old and die in the time it took a spaceship to get us from here to anywhere comparable to here. If the ship did go fast enough to cover any impressive distance in what little time we have, it would need to have a hull that would withstand countless meteor impacts at incredibly high speeds.

Humanity is metaphorically alone on a road in the middle of the Nevada desert, literally running low on gas while we collectively watch the temperature gauge steadily climb. We have less time on this planet every day, and the next service station is over six trillion miles away.

If that isn't a thought that hurts to think, I don't know what is. Which is the other reason this chapter came last: how do you top the knowledge that we are surrounded by peril at all times, both from our planet and from the simple fact that we live on one?

Also, I wanted to let you savor the buildup. You knew this one was coming, and the last thing you needed to do was hit paydirt halfway through the book. Now read the last few pages, please; then figure out which one of my books or blogs you want to read next.

Dear Reader,

This all started as an idea for a book, turned into a fun weekly blog, and finally ended up being both a lot more fun and way more open-ended than I initially anticipated. The blog went from one year to three as soon as I saw how many of these ideas kept popping into my head; and the book was either going to be one giant volume or several small ones.

Well, a couple years back I ran into this problem with my 'Zombie Zero' project. The main story was very much about how nature itself can play a role in making sure humans don't go too far in any dangerous direction, and 'The First Zombie' and 'The Last Zombie' were the only two books I needed to write to tell that story. However, the whole time I was writing I kept seeing other interesting ideas pop up. I found myself wondering more than once how some minor character in the main story got to that place, or where they went from there.

I realized pretty quickly that I wanted to write eighteen of these character prequels and prologues, and I also wanted to figure out the best way to get them into print. We ended up with six short story volumes with three stories each, printed using a trim size small enough to fit in a pocket or purse. They reminded me of the pulp fiction publications I carried around in my back pocket when I was a kid, which was exactly what I had been hoping for. People who bought them loved the size and shape, and right away I started thinking of what else could be best expressed through that format.

If you are reading this as an ebook, you may not know where I'm going with all this; but those of you who bought print copies are right there with me already. I couldn't be more excited about offering this project within this framework, and the subject matter seems perfect for a book formatted small enough to easily carry around with you. There was a time when this might have been the kind of book you recommend people read in the bathroom, but that isn't the sort of thing publishers advise any more.

That being said, you can keep your copy wherever you want.

May I suggest the coffee table, like I did in the foreword? To reiterate, books can be a great way to find the thinkers in the room; and this one in particular is sure to be a conversation starter. Don't think I don't thoroughly understand the introverted life; I'm a writer, after all.

Of all the things I might ask you to do right now so we can get to know each other a little better, one stands out as most important. I have a secret society, which is really just a fancy name for a newsletter. That's the best place to find out about new releases and sales, and I am always sharing something special every week exclusively with my subscribers.

So…do me a favor, if you don't want this to be the last thing you read from me. Sign up for the 'Secret Society of Deeper Meaning' and choose how often you would like to hear from me. If you are reading this as an ebook, you can just click that link.

If you are reading this as a print title, that's even better! You are reading it in the format I intended; which may or may not be important to you, but it really does matter to me. I'm going to ask you to grab your nearest internet enabled device, and go to JayNorry.com. Look around for a little while, and in about a minute the link to join the newsletter will pop up; or you can find the secret society page, and click 'join'.

Without readers, even the most eloquent author is just shouting into an empty void. I would like to tell you how much it means to hear from someone who enjoyed one of my books or blog posts, but that's one of those few places where words fail me. Writing down your ideas and being happy with the way you phrased it is one thing; knowing you are reaching readers who feel like you struck a chord is quite another. Thanks to the efforts of my wife, I have gone from being one kind of author to the other; and I feel a great deal of gratitude for that transition.

And now, I get to hand it to my readers. They are some of my favorite people, after all. I give all my secret society members my email address at the end of each message, and the ability to respond by simply clicking 'reply'. I can't honestly say no email has gone without response, but I can say that almost every message gets a reply. I am so touched whenever I find out someone loved reading something I wrote, at the very least I spend a few minutes in a happy daze of giddiness.

So...if you'd like, join the secret society, let me know what you think about all this, and extend me the wonderful privilege of keeping you up on all things me. I've already written a pretty nice little collection of books, but you can be sure there are a lot more on the way. Also...if you liked this one in particular, you will hopefully be pleased to know there will be several more volumes over the next couple years.

I sure would like it if you join me on those adventures, too; but for now, I'll end this knowing you know I'm grateful to you for reading this book. I hope you enjoyed reading it as much as I loved writing it, and that you maybe feel like you made a new friend somewhere on this lonely old planet floating out here in space.

Thanks for reading!

All the best,
Jay

Also available from Jay Norry. . .

Stumbling Backasswards Into the Light

As J.K. Norry

Dreaming the Perpetual Dream

The Ringer series

Ringing in a Voyage

Ringing in a New Year

Zombie Zero

Zombie Zero: The First Zombie

Zombie Zero: The Last Zombie

Zombie Zero: The Short Stories, Volumes 1-6

The Walking Between Worlds trilogy

Demons & Angels (Book I)

Rise of the Walker King (Book II)

Fall of the Walker King (Book III)

Learn more about Jay at
www.JayNorry.com

Sign up for the Secret Society of Deeper Meaning to get exclusive content, the weekly newsletter, and much more
http://eepurl.com/T3NdD

www.ingramcontent.com/pod-product-compliance
Lightning Source LLC
Chambersburg PA
CBHW051702180726
48283CB00004B/1172

* 9 7 8 1 9 4 4 9 1 6 7 2 5 *